To my friend Michael —
life is t
never kn...
soul will cross our paths !
I'm glad you did... ☺

Much love,
Kristen Brown

Oct. 30
2014

From Doormat to
Sweet Empowerment

A spiritual guide to reclaiming your
personal power in relationships and life

Kristen Brown

BALBOA
PRESS

A DIVISION OF HAY HOUSE

Balboa Press books may be ordered through booksellers or by contacting:

Balboa Press
A Division of Hay House
1663 Liberty Drive
Bloomington, IN 47403
www.balboapress.com
1 (877) 407-4847

Because of the dynamic nature of the Internet, any web addresses or links contained in this book may have changed since publication and may no longer be valid. The views expressed in this work are solely those of the author and do not necessarily reflect the views of the publisher, and the publisher hereby disclaims any responsibility for them.

The author of this book does not dispense medical advice or prescribe the use of any technique as a form of treatment for physical, emotional, or medical problems without the advice of a physician, either directly or indirectly. The intent of the author is only to offer information of a general nature to help you in your quest for emotional and spiritual well-being. In the event you use any of the information in this book for yourself, which is your constitutional right, the author and the publisher assume no responsibility for your actions.

Any people depicted in stock imagery provided by Thinkstock are models, and such images are being used for illustrative purposes only.
Certain stock imagery © Thinkstock.

Printed in the United States of America.

ISBN: 978-1-4525-1903-6 (sc)
ISBN: 978-1-4525-1905-0 (hc)
ISBN: 978-1-4525-1904-3 (e)

Library of Congress Control Number: 2014913093

Balboa Press rev. date: 10/01/2014

DEDICATION

To my mother, Annaliese Gaun and step-father, Guiseppe Candela: You took us in and enfolded us in your loving care and attention. You provided a home and space for me to heal my wounded soul so I could guide my children to empowerment right along with me. Your selflessness and unconditional love has never gone unnoticed nor will it ever. You will forever be my earth angels. I love you.

To my father, Harry Gaun: You are the epitome of "still waters run deep". What emotions you don't show outwardly, come through loud and clear through your unwavering support of me, your beloved grandchildren and the rest the family. You gave my mind rest in times of great strain by relieving burdens I thought I had to carry alone. I am forever grateful for your continual support of my evolution and my family. I love you.

To my children, Sydney, Brody and Remy: I can't even write this dedication without tears filling my eyes. You three have filled my heart with love beyond comprehension! I dedicate this book to you because without your well-being and emotional health as my goal, I'm not sure I would be where I am today. Each and every day, I thank God for you. You have taught me so much about being a good mother and have mirrored back the places I needed to see myself in order to gain a better perspective. I love you.

And last but never least…

To my dearest friends, Sherry Espinosa, Craig Bartels, Amy Joon, Ashley Anderson, Doug Galle, and Sue Markovitch: I have never in my life been so incredibly blessed with such an amazing tribe! The countless hours you listened to me as I ran through my thoughts, emotions, insights, intuitions, ideas, epiphanies, worries and triumphs is priceless! You shared your time with me when I needed it most. You ARE my "supportive community" and not one day goes by that I don't value and understand how fortunate I am for your love and friendship. I am beyond honored to hold you so close to my heart. I love you.

Contents

Foreword

I was a lost soul. I spent many years stuck in self destructive patterns and awful, unhealthy relationships. I would look around at other people and try to understand why they were able to have healthy relationships but I was not. I'd been to a lot of therapy. I understood my losses and my wounds. But I didn't understand how to translate that into a happy, healthy life.

I was stuck. I knew that if I kept repeating the same pattern, I would get the same result. But I didn't know how to change. I kept looking for that thing *out there* that I could get my hands on to get some control over my life so it would finally be different. But that didn't work. All that did was keep the focus outside of myself.

Then I looked within.

What I found was a deep sense of unacceptance of myself and my past. I began to understand that because of that lack of self-love, I was wearing a mask made to gain as much approval as possible. I was performing for acceptance. My life, at its root, lacked integrity. The consequence of that led me to give away much of my personal power and authenticity out of fear; fear of not being good enough, fear of being rejected, and fear of being abandoned.

Looking at and admitting that to myself was not easy. However, owning it was the first step in creating an empowered life. I learned that if I was willing to own it, I could change it. I was indeed a doormat. I had played a role in all the brokenness around me. And that was the best news ever. Finally, I wasn't wishing and waiting in desperation for someone else to change. It was my turn. It was me.

I thoroughly relate to the characteristics of doormathood, such as always putting others first, lack of healthy boundaries, giving myself away for love, and being too afraid to stand up for myself. Kristen Brown nails it in this book when she describes these characteristics. It was validating for me to see my healing journey in the pages of this radically honest, encouraging book. I suddenly felt like instead of traveling this path alone, I had a sister to walk the path with me.

Kristen Brown is that sister of encouragement and support to all of us. She tells it like it is, courageously shares the darkest times in her own story, and leads the way with her very bright light. She reveals the lies that we were stuck within, and she brings the truth about self love and acceptance to light in a way that helps us all, every single one of us recovering doormats, to truly understand that complete healing is possible and there is a way to wholeness.

The way is sweet empowerment. And the how-to that we've all been seeking is revealed in this book in a way that is absolutely doable and life changing. I love that it begins with connecting to our own divinity and the source of love itself. I didn't want to have to conjure up loving feelings for myself. I had tried that many times. I needed help. I believe we all do. And you will find that help in the pages of this incredible book. It is our road map out of doormathood to a life of integrity, healthy relationships and the sweet empowerment we've been dreaming about.

Sue Markovitch
Author of, *I Know What to Do, I Just Don't Do It*
Westerville, Ohio

Introduction

My Dearest Readers,

After I experienced a deeply profound betrayal and upset in my life that started in August of 2009, I made the conscious, dedicated, directed decision to claim victory over my circumstance. I set course to heal and not only did I heal, my entire life began to transform right before my eyes. I learned how my false beliefs about myself and my past behavioral patterns were creating repeating, negative scenarios in my life. I discovered that the only power we have is the power to change ourselves no matter what anyone has done or is doing to us. I awakened to a higher consciousness, a deeper connection to Source and my soul's calling. I call this new awareness "awakening to self-worth."

Although I have always been a "seeker", it was a distinct two year period of time that awakened me to the understanding of how we can claim our worth and personal power at any given time if we fully commit to do so. Even though I continue to evolve every day, I call those specific two years "The College of Kristen" because not unlike academic college, they were a time of concentrated learning, struggle, fear, balance and evolution. It's important to know and understand that it does not have to take a major life crisis to break you open or redirect your path! You can make that decision right here, right now!

I call *From Doormat to Sweet Empowerment* a spiritual guide, because I refer to a Higher Power often. I interchange what I call this Power throughout the text because in my estimation, there really is no name that embodies all of what He/She is. I will use names such as: God, Spirit, Holy Spirit, Source, Source Energy, Universe, Universal Intelligence, Loving Essence and Higher Power. Please understand that with any name I use, I am always referring to the Superpower of the universe as I know and understand it… All Loving and All Good. I believe we co-create our experience with this Energy to learn love, compassion and forgiveness and to live more peacefully while we make manifest our desires. I believe that God/Source/Spirit is pure love and anything outside of that is illusion/fear/ego. When I refer to our "Higher Self", I am referring to the times we are connected to Source, our Light within, Truth. When I use the term "lower self", I am referring to the times we are identifying with our egoic, smaller mind - the fearful disclaimer that tries to sabotage our expansion and healing. You can also choose to view the Higher Self and lower self as the proverbial angel on one shoulder and the devil on the other. I don't claim to be a guru or master of anything nor do I claim to know all there is to know about this Power. I only know that through experience and trial, It is real and here to guide us on our journey.

Chapter One is the only purposefully placed chapter in this book because *Connecting With [My] Divinity* is where my transformation began. In this chapter I share my personal story to better acquaint you with whom I am, where I've been and how my transformation from doormat to empowerment began. After Chapter One, feel free to read the chapters in any order that speaks to you. Honor your soul by doing what feels right and true for you. This is your journey. The concepts and ideas of each chapter were all congruent themes running at the same time during my healing. I didn't stop one to begin another. Additionally, they are the exact same concepts and ideas I continue to practice and strengthen in myself each and every day. Each concept aligns with adopting a new way of thinking, feeling, acting and being that is consistent and supportive of self-love and self-worth. You might also notice that some material might tend to overlap. This is because all the models within are directly connected by the same universal laws. I believe without a doubt that when we love ourselves *first*, *wholly* and *Holy*, all else falls into place. When our highest value becomes our well-being, our life begins to shift in the most fascinating, unexpected and wonderful ways. The path to empowerment is all about changing oneself first in order to create change in one's life.

The stories and excerpts within are true life situations of my own, my coaching/mentoring clients, my friends and family. All names have been changed in order to protect and respect the privacy of others. This book was written to spread light, awareness and to promote healing to its readers. Although I now passionately teach the wisdom and knowledge I've acquired, I continue daily to learn, grow and expand my consciousness. Self-love and personal empowerment is not a destination; it is a way of living.

My invitation to you is to read the content of this book with an open mind and heart. Be willing to discover, uncover and own what is yours to learn and grow from and discard anything that does not ring true in your soul. You might identify with every word in every chapter or we may have been brought together to validate a change you are already in process of. Whatever your purpose for being here is, know it is correct and perfect for you at this time. You found this book (or this book found you) for a Divine reason. There are no coincidences.

The greatest step we can ever make regarding our personal well-being and healing is the first one! I honor the seeker in you and bow to your quest to improve the quality of your life and relationships. I will not give you the false impression it will always be easy. The journey to empowerment will take courage, commitment and time. The fact that you are here, however, tells me you are ready to transform your life and reclaim your personal power, confidence and joy. Taking the first step in *any recovery* is the hardest and you have already done it! I honor and congratulate you!

In closing, always remember that life is a process. Change is a process. Be gentle with yourself while on your journey. Stay your course, encourage and congratulate yourself often and most importantly honor yourself for the beautiful, unique soul that you are!

With love,
Kristen Brown

Chapter One

Connect With Your Divinity

"Whenever we feel lost, or insane, or afraid, all we have to do is ask for His help. The help might not come in the form we expected or even thought we desired, but it will come, and we will recognize it by how we feel. In spite of everything, we will feel at peace."
– Marianne Williamson

When I began putting this book together, I knew there was only one chapter that was apropos for Chapter One. My journey to personal empowerment and the reclaiming of my life all began here with the foundation of connecting with my Divinity. The information, wisdom and lessons I learned and continue to strengthen in myself, all started when I began letting go of self-perceived limitations of my ego (lower self) and began attaching to and trusting the messages and guidance I received from my Higher Self and God. I learned how Love heals all and fear perpetuates pain. I began to embrace our true Essence- as individual aspects of God- and started living within that truth. I found peace in extreme circumstance and my path to empowerment began. In this chapter, I share my story, the spiritual awakening that followed, and how I learned the power of surrender, forgiveness and the transformation of suffering into peace.

My Tsunami – Where it began

In October 2003, I met a man who appeared to be a gift from heaven. He was bright, kind, funny, intelligent and ambitious. He seemed to accept my two children from a previous marriage as his own and I couldn't help but feel like I won the lottery. I married him in September 2005. My children had grown to love and admire him tremendously and even opted to call him "Dad". He was an aspiring jet pilot still at the bottom of his career and not yet bringing in a substantial income. However, I was at the top of my career, a homeowner, a business owner and quite financially secure. Naturally, I became the bread winner in the family and continued to for the majority of our six years together. I supported and loved my husband financially and emotionally without condition.

Five years into our relationship, my husband got a position as a captain on a personal jet for an oil tycoon whose home base was Nigeria, Africa. His "tours" were five to six weeks working and five weeks off. His total days away from home would equal close to half a year. Prior to this career move, we had had a daughter together. With two preteens, a new baby, working full-time and a husband who was absent a lot, it goes without saying that I was exhausted. With his new position, he had morphed into the bread winner of the family and I agreed to give up my career as a successful hairstylist to stay home in order to focus on the children and our affairs. I relinquished the clientele I had accrued for over 19 years and officially retired at 42. It was bittersweet to say the least, but I felt at the time it was the right thing for our family.

While on tour, my husband vacillated between loving emails laden with tears of sadness for missing his family to the extreme opposite behavior of ignoring all texts and phone calls from me for sometimes the entire duration of his absence. His behavior became very confusing and a great source of stress and pain. The man I trusted and loved was morphing into a very different and unrecognizable person right before my eyes. I was very confused and afraid. I would try to discuss his odd behaviors only to be met with silence, avoidance or him turning it around on me somehow.

Fast forward to August 2009, several months after settling into my new role of stay-at-home mom, my husband Skyped me on his eighth day of tour, and I believe the words he said were, *"I'm going to get an apartment when I get home."* Due to the extreme amounts of emotional turmoil I had been living in, my response was simply, *"Okay, if you're sure this is what you want to do."* In my soul, I knew there was something very dark going on inside of him and I was powerless to help him. I wondered if perhaps this might be just what he needed in order to redefine his life and priorities. I was willing to give him the break he requested and continue to co-parent along the way. When he returned home from tour, he promptly rented a $2000/month fully furnished apartment in a gated community. Out of his six months lease, he spent approximately fifteen days there. Instead, he chose to stay in Africa on his off weeks. Additionally, he cut all contact with me and he began withholding a large portion of the money he agreed to give me monthly to cover our mortgage and bills. He claimed he had other expenses now. Things got financially tight very quickly. I could feel the Titanic starting to sink and panic was quickly descending upon me.

To this day he has not had any personal or direct contact with any of us including his little girl. Needless to say we were all shocked and devastated by his betrayal. The mess he left for me to clean up was overwhelming at best. I was left with a huge house that I needed to sell quickly, a relocation of schools, court proceedings, the physical and emotional needs of three children and the biological abandonment of our little one who quickly developed severe separation anxiety when anyone she loved attempted to leave the house. All the aforementioned stresses were overshadowed with my own overwhelming emotional distress of having zero financial means to support my family. One might ask why I didn't immediately go back to work. The answer is: I had passed my clientele on to other stylists leaving them with no hope or expectation of me ever returning back to this career. In the hair styling world, once clients get reestablished and begin forming new relationships with another stylist, they stay put. Additionally, hair styling is not something you can jump back into and make the same income you were immediately. It is a client building career which takes approximately 3 years (in a good economy) to build a profitable business. Additionally, this situation happened during one of the biggest economic slumps we have faced as Americans since the Great Depression. Salon revenue across the board was suffering terribly and has still not yet returned to what is used to be. Finding gainful employment with my skill set to support our needs was impossible. A minimum wage job wouldn't even begin to scratch the surface. I was in a terribly desperate situation with literally no quick or easy way out.

My panic was increasing every day. This was absolutely the most frightening situation I had ever encountered. *How on earth was I going to support my children?!* I felt raped of any and all security I had. If it wasn't for the loving charity of my parents who took us in, we would have literally been homeless. My self-esteem, my self-image, my emotional and financial security, my identity and my dreams were gone. All that I had known, all that I had worked for, all that made me feel safe in this world, was swept away in one gigantic wave of betrayal. That is why I refer to this time as "my tsunami". Additionally, I had nothing in form (the material world) that I could identify with to promote a sense of security, identity or belonging. I was no longer a wife, financially secure, a homeowner or a business owner. My identity was shattered. It was complete and utter devastation. Everything was gone. What had taken decades to accomplish was wiped out. Feelings of helplessness and despair overwhelmed my life. I was caught in the current of obsessive thinking, worry and anxiety. My situation was completely out of my control and I felt like I would explode into a million pieces at any moment. I had no idea how I was ever going to recover from this. Writing this still brings tears to my eyes as I reflect upon the helpless feeling I had about being unable to emotionally and financially care for my children. It was the fear beyond all fears for me.

I am blessed for the small few who spent many tireless hours talking to and loving me. Although their love and kindness was selfless and beautiful, as soon as I would hang up the phone or leave their company, my downward spiral would begin again. The betrayal was so great and the mess I was left in so utterly astounding, nothing truly served as long term comfort. I couldn't eat, I lost quite a bit of weight and had a terrible time staying focused on any one task no matter how minute. I spent a lot of time sitting alone and staring into space. I was frozen, shattered and depleted. I had never felt more insecure or frightened in my entire life and I had no idea where to turn or what to do next. I remember identifying with how devastating life experiences can ruin people forever and how staying stuck in one's story of victimhood could be quite easy. I was on a slippery slope.

Remembering God

"In that Holy Place where you tell Him everything and he understands; there are angels who stand in wait to hear his every command. How may they serve you and increase your joy." -Marianne Williamson

"Where there is lack, God's abundance is on the way. Hold on. Have faith. It's coming." -Marianne Williamson

Through my dazed and confused mind, I slowly recognized that I was the only person who truly had the power to release me from this emotional prison and I needed to find a way soon! I knew deep inside it was all up to me and I was profoundly weary. I kept trudging forward even though I felt like I had only a mere fingertip on faith. My thoughts were ruling my mind. *How was I ever going to recover from this devastation? How will I ever be able to provide for my children while I am rebuilding my clientele? I will always have to depend on my parents. I will be alone and broke forever. How did this happen to me? I don't deserve this! I gave everything to him!* And on and on they went. If it was a negative, defeating thought, I guarantee I was thinking it. I was hanging by a thread dangling over an abyss so deep, that if I succumbed I may have been lost forever. I had so many unanswered questions and "whys?" that sometimes it was not even feasible to believe I would come out of this at all, let alone come out of this powerfully.

It was my love for my children and their emotional and physical well-being that became my driving force. I knew that I had to "get right" or I was not going to be able to bring them through this successfully. I searched for a feasible answer, but there simply wasn't one. And then... I remembered God. I found my courageous warrior within and I made the unmovable decision that I was *not* going to live as a victim. I decided to fight for my life and the well-being of my children no matter how hard it was or how long it took. I didn't know how this would look or how on Earth I was going to do it, but I chose victory over victimhood. I chose God. I kept my eye on the tiny tidbit of faith I had and began to pray and meditate as often as I could. I had always believed in a Higher Power, I just didn't know how high or how powerful He/She is. It was time for me to find out.

In my moments of stillness (and only in stillness), a gentle guiding voice would speak. My inner knowing began to resound in my mind like a clear and powerful guide. I understood *completely* and with no question that I had to take the one fingertip I had on faith and cultivate it into a full body explosion of Light. I needed God now more than ever and I was going to trust in all that I had believed this Power to be. I understood, perhaps for the first time, that I cannot do it alone. I fell to my knees (opened my heart) and I asked for help.

Waking Up – The College of Kristen

"No one and nothing outside of you can give you salvation, or free you from the misery. You have to light your own lamp. You have to know the miniature universe that you yourself are." -Banani Ray

In my quest for healing, I read every spiritual, self-help book I could get my hands on. I watched endless spiritual and uplifting videos and listened to preachers, speakers and philosophers of all types. My two older children would often joke with me, *"Oh man, you're watching Joel Osteen again?!" (At that time, I considered Joel Osteen my personal cheerleader!)* I was thirsty for any inspiration, hope or wisdom I could find. I highlighted lines and quotes in my books and I began journaling about my feelings and inner guidance. I treated my healing much like getting a college degree. I had found a "new thought" church some years earlier and I began attending every Sunday. I could hardly make it through the inspirational talk without publicly sobbing. I did everything I could do to stay in touch with Source Energy and strengthen my faith. I knew the only way out of this pain was through Divine Guidance and I became obsessed with finding my healing and peace.

The awakening was slow at first, but as time progressed, I began to catch tiny glimpses of sunlight streaming through the dark, storm clouds of my life. No matter how minute the glimpses were, I took them as previews to the blue sky that inevitably always follows a storm. Even though my hope was shaky at best, through finite notice of this tiny ray of light my hope began to grow. In those moments I would pause to **feel** the victory as if I already had it. I slowly began waking up to the unconditional love and the infinite possibilities of the Universe. Even in the midst of extreme chaos, emotional pain and physical upheaval, I *knew* and *felt* on some unexplainable, cosmic level that this situation was happening *for* me and not *to* me. What was presenting to me in the natural (material world) looked beyond restoration, but I knew/felt somewhere in the deepest part of my soul, that my children and I were not only going to be okay, but we were going to be better than ever! I didn't know how it was going to happen, but I trusted it.

Even though my goal started out to merely get through this horrific situation and regain my footing, what came to be in the years that followed was nothing short of extraordinary. I opened my heart to a new and improved thought system and an abundance of possibilities. My mind and spirit expanded. I began to explore brand new perspectives that I never knew existed. The storm clouds were most definitely clearing! I started *to feel... to open... to forgive...to love...to listen... to compassion... to humble... to grow... to learn... and mostly... to heal.* When I began to open my heart, my life began to change and a series of synchronicities and miracles followed. Oftentimes, I just stood in awe as it all perfectly unfolded around me. I was learning the art of surrendering to God and witnessing firsthand the power behind it.

I used to be a person who only called on God when I was in pain and desperation. *Dear God, the going is really rough here! Please help me out!* I began to wonder why I had only reached for God when I was struggling. I opened to the idea that God was not just a sometimes thing. God is omnipresent. He/She is not only available 9-5 Monday through Friday, closed evenings and weekends nor does one need an appointment to connect. Source Energy runs in and through all things at all times. It's a 24-7-365 deal! I learned to invite this Loving Essence into my life all day every day. I began a morning prayer/meditation ritual and I reminded myself to return to God several times throughout the day for peace and comfort. It was not always easy; however, I knew *I* was the only chance I had and I kept my attention on my intention: peace and healing.

My daily mantra/prayer:

Holy Spirit, Fill me up with your goodness and love today so I may operate within this loving space and make decisions from my Highest Self regarding me and my children. I am open to receiving your Divine guidance and wisdom. May I bring Light and love to all I encounter this day. Amen.

This is when the miracle happened. When my energy shifted, my whole world began shifting. I began to show up differently in the world even in the midst of chaos and upheaval. I began transforming into a more peaceful, centered and confident person. I noticed a *stillness, a peace* appearing in my soul and consequently, my life, like never before. The love that *I am* started to emanate outward and I found myself attracting in wonderful and fascinating new people, opportunities and experiences. I was in awe of the peace that was enveloping my life. My thoughts were:

Was it really this easy? Is this what was missing from my life all along? Had I misunderstood Who/What God is? To finally understand that this is what it meant to be connected to my Divinity was priceless. To think how I had lived for so long only calling on God in times of distress was foolish. I now knew that reclaiming my Essence, my life and myself, was a daily and sometimes moment by moment practice.

Connecting to God led me to discover a deeper meaning to the words peace, love, forgiveness, tolerance, faith, abundance and healing. I started to understand things on a different level. What I had always felt in the recesses of my being became visible in my conscious mind. I learned the power of surrender and allowing the Universe to handle any matter at hand in the best possible way. When we truly surrender to a Higher Will, it is not long until we begin to witness the Divine perfection in everything as it unfolds. The doubt that once shadowed our minds becomes illuminated with Light and we begin to *see...* perhaps for the very first time! We begin to awaken to the only thing that is real- Love- and we finally learn to trust in a power greater than ourselves.

Surrender

"When we surrender to God, we surrender to something bigger than ourselves - to a universe that knows what It's doing. When we stop trying to control events, they fall into a natural order, an order that works. We're at rest while a power much greater than our own takes over, and it does a much better job than we could have done. We learn to trust that the power that holds galaxies together can handle the circumstances of our relatively little lives. Surrender means, by definition, giving up attachment to results. When we surrender to God, we let go of our attachment to how things happen on the outside and we become more concerned with what happens on the inside. Something amazing happens when we surrender and just love. We melt into another world, a realm of power already within us. The world changes when we change. The world softens when we soften. The world loves us when we choose to love the world." -Marianne Williamson

One of the greatest and most powerful gifts we can ever give to ourselves is the power of surrender - to let go and let God. When I finally understood that I was not alone and that the Universe had my back, I was able to settle back into the unknown a little more comfortably. It actually felt like a tremendous relief to know that I did not have to do this alone! I felt that there was no better place for my worries than to hand them over to a Power that saw the bigger picture and knew exactly how to move the pieces of my life into alignment with victory. Anytime I began to feel overwhelmed with obsessive worry, I would take a moment to focus on a practice I call, *"Give it to God."* I would sit quietly and visualize myself wrapping up each worry in a beautiful package adorned with a stunning bow and send it into the Universe much like one would release a helium balloon to the atmosphere. I would watch each package until it eventually faded from view. I would then trust with all of my being that God had me and everything was going to work out for the Highest Good for all. Through this visualization practice, I would feel a tremendous burden lift from my shoulders and my heart would expand.

At times, it was easier said than done, but I knew how much pressure it released for me, so I kept to it no matter how long it took to feel the release. I was diligent with my practice. I would repeat and repeat the visualization until I literally **felt** like I was truly giving my problems away to someone who could handle them better. To live in the illusion that we have *complete* control, only promotes and prolongs our suffering. However, the things we do have control over are our thoughts, perceptions, beliefs, behaviors and our free-will to invite Source into our lives daily to restore us back to sound mind. I remember clearly the concept I learned in *Return to Love* by Marianne Williamson where she explained that we are likely to let God handle the less significant worries, but the ones we are more deeply attached to or believe are more important, we feel we have to control ourselves. She explained how all worries are created equal to God. That there is no order of difficulty for Universal Resource and God is equipped to handle the bigger things just are readily as He/She is equipped to handle the smaller things.

I also began reinforcing my faith in divine timing. Divine timing understands that nothing happens before its time and it will happen for the Highest Good of all concerned. Although, oftentimes it won't look the way we *think* it should. We can fret and worry and try to manipulate circumstance, but it will not change the Divine plan. I began to understand that by attempting to control, manipulate or speed up outcome, it could actually prolong what was trying to come to me. I could potentially muddy the waters (interfering) and/ or adding more confusion to a situation that was just becoming clear.

Eight months after our separation, my husband and I were to appear in court to determine the monetary issues of our divorce. Since I have never had to testify in court, I had no idea what to expect. Being my family's financial livelihood and future was at stake, I was beginning to reel with anxiety. Sitting outside the courtroom, I sat in quiet meditation and fully surrendered the outcome to God's Divine Will. I remember being fascinated at how quiet and centered I was as I entered the stand and prepared for questioning. After two days of testimony on both sides, court was adjourned. We were informed the ruling would come via postal mail and would take approximately 30 days. I continued my meditation and surrender practice. *It will be what it will be. All will be in Divine Right Order.* When the court document appeared in the mail, I was very nervous to read it. With a pounding heart, I had to read through the legal jargon several times before fully grasping its meaning. And then I understood… The judge had ruled in my favor.

Through our Suffering, We Find Peace

"Without suffering, you cannot grow. Without suffering, you cannot get the peace and joy you deserve. Please don't run away from your suffering. Embrace it and cherish it… With understanding and compassion, you will be able to heal the wounds in your heart, and the wounds in the world… Our suffering has the capacity of showing us the path to liberation. Embrace your suffering, and let it reveal to you the way to peace."
–Thich Nhat Hanh

It has been said by many spiritual teachers that after a total devastation of life is experienced (suffering) and all that one may have known and attached to in the material world is gone, is a person then humble and open enough to receive a higher consciousness. That only through the suffering is he or she truly ready to tap into the essence of Source that is in and through us all. It is through this return to Love, that we find our sanity and like a Phoenix rising from the ashes, we are restored even more brilliant and powerful than we were before. What initially may have been viewed as wreckage and demolition was later revealed as a pathway leading us to Truth, healing and spiritual evolution.

Suffering can help us to strengthen our spiritual muscle and build faith in knowledge and understanding that all is in Divine Right Order. That a Power greater than us can and will lead us to peace and victory if we surrender and open our hearts to it. It is within this very awareness that we finally expand our vision and open our eyes to the majestic power and creative forces working behind the scenes. We learn to stop trying to control, control, control, and instead work in unity with our Source to lead us to our best possible outcome. We finally awaken to *seeing/feeling/hearing/knowing* what has always been available (Source Energy) and infinite possibilities become our life's theme.

However, with that being said, it does not have to take full devastation to claim our Divine Nature. At any time, we can tap into our Source and begin to co-create a life of healing, forgiveness and abundance. We can choose at any moment to grow from our suffering-large or small. As the well-known Buddhist monk, Thich Nhat Hanh, once said, *"People suffer because they are caught in their views. As soon as we release those views, we are free and we don't suffer anymore."* At any moment in our lives we can turn suffering into peace. We can realize how the best possible outcomes run congruent with the connection, support and love of God and when we consciously choose Love over fear, God over ego, we find our peace.

Forgiveness

> *"The process of healing is all about forgiveness."*
> –Debbie Ford

> *"Never succumb to the temptation of bitterness."*
> -Martin Luther King Jr.

Choosing forgiveness is to understand completely that forgiveness is solely about you and not the other person. It is the knowing that holding onto hatred, bitterness and/or anger does not poison our enemy, it poisons us. Forgiveness is a releasing of toxic energy from the mind, body and spirit. It is choosing Light over darkness every time we are done wrong. Mohandas Gandhi once said, *"The weak can never forgive. Forgiveness is an attribute of the strong."* In choosing forgiveness, we work toward keeping our hearts open and our minds clear in order to move forward in life with empowerment and confidence. Forgiveness is not always easy and may oftentimes feel like the harder path to take. It takes fortitude and courage to be in charge of our own thoughts and emotions thus choosing our own experience every day. When we forgive, we are dissolving the emotional link (bitterness and anger) that has kept or keeps us connected to our offender. We choose to see the innocence of their behavior and we allow their punishment to be what it will be. We may not ever get to see their karma returned, but we can rest knowing God has this. With forgiveness, we are choosing personal freedom over self-imprisonment.

One might believe that non-forgiveness gives us control or authority over another person's life and that non-forgiveness holds him/her accountable for his actions. To believe this is an illusion. Our perpetrator will continue to live his life and lie to himself through mental justifications of his actions no matter what. I assure you, he is not going to hold himself back just because *you* haven't forgiven him. Unless or until he has a major epiphany or has a profound spiritual awakening, the justifications and lies will continue throughout his lifetime with little or no thought about whether you have forgiven him or not. Our un-forgiveness won't magically lead our wrong-doers to Light. To live in contempt and hatred only darkens your soul, not your perpetrator's.

Our lack of forgiveness for another does not impose any punishment on the perpetrator- it only punishes us.

It is important to note that forgiveness is *not* about condoning another's bad behavior. It does not mean we are letting the other person off the hook. Martin Luther King once said, *"The Lord never said I had to like my enemies."* Amen to that. Forgiveness does not mean we agree with another's behavior or are inviting the person back into our lives. Forgiveness is about duly noting the wrong doing, releasing the emotional burden of carrying it and then choosing an appropriate action or boundary if needed. Just because we choose forgiveness, does not mean we have to continue to subject ourselves to that sort of immoral character in the future. Forgiveness is about our own personal freedom. Freedom to live without added emotional weight, freedom to take back our power and freedom to choose whom we allow in our lives.

God's Business

"May we not succumb to thoughts of violence and revenge today, but rather to thoughts of mercy and compassion. We are to love our enemies that they might be returned to their right minds."
–Marianne Williamson

What others do in their lives is God's business, not ours. God knows exactly when His/Her children stray and furthermore, He/She knows what each of us needs in order to learn and grow. It is not up to us to play God. We are minute in comparison to the infinite intelligence of the Universe and we simply do not have the power to handle it. "I have faith in God" is not just a pretty little sentence we get to say in order to convince ourselves we are okay. Peace comes when we *truly believe* with every fiber of our entire being and body that *God has this*. Our job right now is to take care of ourselves best so that we may show up in our lives and for our beloveds in the highest possible way. Part of excellent self-care is reclaiming one's personal power through and with the practice of forgiveness.

However, with that being said, there is something we can do for the other person. We can send him love so that he may be returned to his Right Mind. I'm sure some of you are thinking… *What?! No way!!* I completely understand that reaction and I gently remind you that that is only your lower self (ego) trying to keep you stuck in the dark with your perpetrator. Thich Nhat Hahn so eloquently stated, *"When another person makes you suffer, it is because he suffers deeply within himself, and his suffering is spilling over. He does not need punishment; he needs help. That's the message he is sending."* I began to understand this on a whole new level. During a second court battle with my ex some two years later over child support modification, lack of medical reimbursements, custody and conditions in our divorce decree he had failed to comply to, I spoke telepathically to him almost every day. Even though what he was doing was unethical and very difficult to swallow, I chose to appeal to the glimmer of Light I knew was underneath his cloak of wounds. I would say:

I know in your heart you love your child and you know I am taking great care of her. Please open your heart during these proceedings so that we may come to a mutually fair agreement so that I may take the best care of our little girl as I can. Please know that when you play fair, my stress is decreased and I can show up for her a better

Momma. I know Who you are and I know what good you are capable of. If/when you heal, you will be welcomed back into her life. Thank you.

I even made a Facebook post asking everyone to *"…send love to a person I am currently dealing with who has strayed to the dark side so that he may feel, for at least a moment, the right thing to do".* Many people were initially shocked at what I was asking for; however, something in their souls understood. Undoubtedly, I was granted the change in his child support obligation and I now receive payment each month on time. And with each payment I receive, I silently and humbly thank him.

How to forgive

"God gives us His strength by giving us His vision of things. Our seeing people as innocent is the only way to achieve God's peace." - Marianne Williamson

Forgiveness is all about release - releasing the misdeeds of others in order to keep ourselves in alignment with Spirit or *at least be willing to try.* It is through this spiritual alignment that we find peace, empowerment and make better choices regarding ourselves and our

From Doormat to Sweet Empowerment

loved ones. I chose forgiveness because I understood that my ex had lost conscious contact with Who he is (a child of God) and was making his choices based on fear, lack of approval, hiding and ego. Most often if we look deep enough into the psyche of our betrayer, we will see a wounded child doing his/her best. Unfortunately, we have become the collateral damage of another's suppressed pain. I like to personify this straying from the Light (God Self) as "Darth Vader". In the blockbuster series *Star Wars*, the character Anakin Skywalker sold his soul to the dark side. Even after living for years an evil man, the Love that was still inside him later saved his son, Luke, from sure death by the Emperor Palpitine. Just because one of God's children has strayed doesn't mean he is beyond healing and redemption.

Marianne Williamson states, *"[Forgiveness] is converting your thinking to a spiritual perspective. You train your mind to be on the look-out for the blessing or the innocence. People tried to do the right thing. It's more than a paradigm shift- it's more of a world view shift."* Forgiveness is a shift in perception where we choose to view another's wrongful behavior through spiritual eyes instead of through the eyes of judgment, condemnation and our lower self. It is knowing that

God will take care of His/Her son and it is not our job. It is about consciously choosing the path of the Holy Spirit as opposed to filling our hearts with darkness. I knew that I had given enough of my energy toward my ex's betrayal and it was time to take my power back. To live and relive his treachery was eating away at my soul. I couldn't function from my Highest Self and the effects of that were showing up in my life. I knew that I could not give or teach my children what I did not have. If I wasn't healed, I couldn't help them to heal.

Allow for the process

Oftentimes I refer to forgiveness as a peeling away the layers of an onion. We may find ourselves feeling pretty good about things then wham! get triggered once more and the whole story comes crashing down again. The good news is, once we gain spiritual ground, we don't go backward. Yes, we may be faced with yet another layer to peel away; however, we must honor how far we've already come. As stated earlier, two years after our divorce, I was back in litigation with my ex. During this time, he even went as far to claim our daughter was not his. This was incredibly painful for me. Not only because he was suggesting I was an adulterer, but he was denying his baby girl's lineage. She still loves and misses him very much and his accusation was a tough pill to swallow. I couldn't help but feel how she would feel if she knew this and it broke my heart. I allowed myself to feel the feelings, vent out my anger and frustration and once again… I chose forgiveness.

With forgiveness, we may think we have completely forgiven and moved on only to then be faced with another level or layer to undo. The process may not be over in one fell swoop. Triggers happen and our stress levels fluctuate, meaning we are weaker at times, thus occasionally causing us to fall headfirst back into our stories. This is not the time to fret. It's the time to get proactive with your forgiveness once again. Our conscious behaviors manifest better effects in our futures. Forgiveness does not go without reward. However, it is oftentimes a silent reward that manifests in glorious ways that may be undetectable to anyone but ourselves. It affects our general well-being, our level of personal peace and our ability to navigate through life unburdened and free.

"Forgiveness is not an occasional act. It is a permanent attitude." – Martin Luther King Jr.

I considered not writing about forgiveness because the subject itself could be its own book. However, truly learning to forgive and practicing it daily, has been a magnificently empowering tool. Through forgiveness one can literally *feel* her power coming back. Forgiveness allows us to keep our hearts open and our minds clear of destructive thoughts and it allows space for our blessings to come into conscious view. It gives us the means to move forward in life without attachment to others' unhealthy behaviors so that we may truly live how God intended - with love, with grace and with connection to Him/Her.

"A queen is wise. She has earned her serenity, not having had it bestowed on her but having passed her tests. She has suffered and grown more beautiful because of it. She has proved she can hold her kingdom together. She has become its vision. She cares deeply about something bigger than herself. She rules with authentic power." –Marianne Williamson

Thoughts to Ponder: *Do I have faith and belief in myself and my Higher Power? Have I invited my Higher Power into my life? Am I willing to open my heart to Divine guidance*

so that I may lead a more pleasing, soul-centered life? Have I chosen forgiveness for those who have wronged me?

Set the Intention: *I am one with God. My true value as a human being is beautifully Divine and on purpose. My value is the Light and Love that I am. I am open to creating with God to bring out my greatness and prosper a life of abundance. And so it is.*

Forgiveness Prayer: *Holy Spirit, I am willing to forgive my wrong-doer because I know to forgive will guide me closer to Truth, harmony, freedom and living a more joyful life. I open my heart to your help. And so it is.*

Chapter Two

Going Within: Inner Dialogue, Forgiveness and Self-love

"True forgiveness demands that we stop beating ourselves up for our mistakes and imperfections and cultivate compassionate self-love instead."
–Debbie Ford

Doormats typically have an underlying bad self-image which stays enriched by a steady stream of negative self-talk, unforgiveness and self-loathing. Our internal chatter can be a subconscious mechanism that has been repeated so long through our conditioned mind that we are quite unaware of the havoc it's causing. We may also notice that our inner critic or "voice" has created a general theme in some, if not all areas in our lives: *I'm not good enough, smart enough, funny enough, attractive enough and so on*. We speak ugly to ourselves (negative inner dialogue), we beat ourselves up (unforgiveness) and we hate ourselves for not being perfect (self-loathing).

When we are unwilling to treat ourselves gently and with compassion, we position ourselves for defeat. How we think about ourselves and treat ourselves is what we become. By becoming aware of our negative inner messages/beliefs/thoughts and transforming them into loving, supportive ones, we naturally begin to show up in the world a more empowered individual. Inner dialogue correction, self-love and forgiveness are **pertinent** in raising our self-esteems and forging a powerful path forward. A centered and nourished deep love and respect of self, has a way of naturally leading us to better positions in life. By creating a shift in our own energy and being, we automatically emit to the world that certain situations and behaviors from others are simply unacceptable. We quit settling for unfavorable conditions and become only willing to be in the presence of individuals of equal or greater vibrational frequency. Our goal in doormat recovery is to love the whole Essence and uniqueness of our personality and core in order to reclaim the personal power in our lives. Through conscious awareness of how we treat ourselves, we can make the crucial shift required to achieving this goal.

All self-empowerment work begins within. It's not about pointing the finger outward, but looking inward. It is about looking at ourselves and what it is about *us* that is allowing or accepting what is happening around us or to us. When we keep the focus off ourselves, we are deterring ourselves from seeing the very things that can and will move and transform us. Oftentimes, those very things are self-love, self-forgiveness and inner dialogue correction. When we shift these things within ourselves, the outside world begins to shift with us. Contrarily, when we sit in righteous indignation, pointing at and focusing on what others are doing, we will only perpetuate the same themes in our life. We cannot change anyone else, no matter how wrong they are so looking outward does us no good. The empowered person knows that she can only change herself and that going within *first* is how she transforms her mind and her life.

Make the Commitment

"Because one believes in oneself, one doesn't try to convince others. Because one is content with oneself, one doesn't need others' approval. Because one accepts oneself, the whole world accepts him or her." -Lao Tzu

When we make a commitment to regain our personal power, we are purposefully and intentionally setting the foundation for a shift in our growth and energy. What we are mindful of, we create. How does a person reach the goal of losing fifty pounds of extra weight? By first making a commitment to it and then fully believing that she can! By holding a mental picture of herself at a healthier weight, everything she does will fall into alignment with this goal. The same goes for personal empowerment. By holding a mental picture of oneself as an empowered, confident person, we not only begin to act in ways to support this goal, but the Universe will do Its part behind the scenes to assist us in reaching it. When we change the energy (thoughts) around a certain subject, we begin the process of manifestation and transformation. When we become conscious of our behaviors and words, change begins. There is no way that it can't. Our thoughts create energy and energy creates movement. Our willingness to speak our truth becomes easier and we are no longer imprisoned by what others think of us. However, the energy shift cannot happen without first a change in perception.

A change in perception creates a change in direction.

Our self-perception cannot and will not change long term if we do not do the work to locate the blocks that perpetuate this ongoing negative cycle. Making a commitment to oneself is one of the first and most powerful steps to reclaiming one's personal power. In this we are telling our souls we matter, we value ourselves and we are committed to doing the work necessary to nurture our hearts and minds so we may heal and evolve. Making this commitment does not mean we freak out and beat ourselves up when we stumble- because we will stumble. Committing to self requires that we are kind and patient with ourselves while recognizing our patterns or mistakes. We treat ourselves gently as we would treat a toddler learning to walk. The first step to committing to self is to finally understand and own the beauty and greatness of Who we really are by bowing to our souls and becoming 100% committed to our healing.

Recognizing Your Inner Dialogue

"The most influential and frequent voice you hear is your inner-voice. It can work in your favor or against you, depending on what you listen to and act upon."
- Maddy Malhotra

Recognizing our self-defeating thoughts can seem very arduous at first and with all personal growth, it is a process that we must be patient with. Our conditioned, repeating thoughts have become deeply ingrained over time and can date as far back as early childhood or an experience that left a mark on our hearts. It is not important to know precisely when the thought or self-judgment happened; however, it is important to observe yourself, so that you can become highly conscious of any and all unserving dialogue. As the recognition occurs, one may become overwhelmed when realizing how terribly mean she has been to herself. She may even begin to feel sad when first discovering this realization. Sounds a little ironic, but it can happen and is definitely something to keep an eye out for. Remember, our goal is not to demean ourselves, but to *simply locate* the defeating thoughts that are causing us pain.

I remember when I first began this process I was absolutely shocked and horrified by my inner-dialogue. I felt so sorry for the recipient (me) of my bullying because I would never say such ugly things to anyone else. How could I be so abusive to myself?! I was mortified! One day in a quiet moment, I decided to apologize to myself. I gave myself the kindest, heartfelt apology I knew how. In that moment, I felt released. I knew I had made a firm commitment to myself and simply through the act of self-apology, years of negative self-image and turmoil began to fall away. I began to feel a sense of safety with myself that I had never known before. For the first time in my life, I felt safe in my own care. How can we ever feel safe in someone's care if they are despicable to us? We can't. The same goes for how we treat ourselves. If we do not feel safe within or trust ourselves, we end up making very bad decisions and allow treatment from others that is not honoring to our souls.

Self-apology begets the same feeling we get when someone we love offers us a sincere, full-ownership apology. Almost immediately the intensity of the wrong-doing loses its strength and love enters the room. At that moment, when one owns his/her stuff, we can feel his/her love and commitment to the relationship and with it comes a sense of security. The same is true when we love ourselves and we are humble enough to say, *"I'm sorry I did this to you."* Years of insecurity seems to decrease in moments.

It is of utmost importance during this time to practice loving kindness with yourself and to remember that you are not alone in this. *There is nothing exclusively wrong with you.* This is an epidemic among people and something that once healed could actually change the world's function on a global level. At this point you are not only working on yourself to end your suffering, but through the collective consciousness of the world, you will be contributing to universal healing.

How to locate and recognize defeating thoughts:

- **Become very conscious of your emotions.** Our emotions serve as beacons to show us where our thoughts are not positive or kind. If we are feeling down or low, chances are there is a negative thought that is causing the upheaval. It's all about chasing the emotion back, one thought at a time, to the originating thought/ belief.

- **Locate the areas in your life where you are putting yourself on hold.** When we hold ourselves back from pursuing our life's desires, there is usually a reason why and most often there is a defeating thought attached to it. As with this whole process, radical self-honesty about your inner-dialogue will lead you directly to your defeating thought.

- **Sit down with a trusted friend or coach.** If you are having difficulty locating your negative dialogue (this can happen from years of mind conditioning), consider sitting down with a trusted friend, coach, counselor or clergy member who is willing to be completely honest with you. If you sit with another people pleaser, chances are he or she will be more concerned with "hurting your feelings" than giving you the candid words that might possibly change your life.

Please remember, the process of defeating thought discovery, is not something that can be skipped over or forgotten. The root of our suffering begins and ends with our thoughts, beliefs and self-lies. Learning to cultivate a loving heart and inner dialogue begins with locating, talking about and turning around each defeating thought. Once we've located the troubled area, it is of *major importance* to get that thought/belief/lie turned around into at least three positive, supporting thoughts that are **as true or truer** than the originating thought. Below is an example of a belief I had to undo. I didn't realize how much havoc it caused in my heart, until I turned it around into a truer statement. Only because of the tremendous relief I felt, did I recognize how painful holding onto the original belief truly was.

Belief/Lie: *I am single and that means there is something wrong with me.*

New thought/Truth: *I am single because I am healing the places in me that historically attracted the wrong type of mate. I would rather be single than in a bad relationship or filling a void I need to learn to fill myself. I am honoring my sacred self and my right match will come.*

"Man is a product of his thoughts. What he thinks he becomes." –Mohandas Gandhi

Love Yourself Wholly and Holy

"Love is the great miracle cure. Loving ourselves works miracles in our lives." –Louise Hay

To love ourselves "wholly" is to embrace all aspects of our unique, authentic nature, gifts, talents, physicality and personality. To love ourselves "Holy" is to honor our Essence (child of God) from the deepest places in our souls. I discovered this miracle organically as I began my healing work. When I started to love myself, my entire being softened. I humbled. I became grateful. My life started to show me how different and better things can be when we shift our inner world. This does not mean, however, that we are becoming selfish. Many clients have expressed to me that when they attempted to do something loving toward self, they always felt it was selfish and inevitably decided not to. It's important to know that to love one's self is not a selfish act. As Louise Hay stated so succinctly in the above quote, "Love is the miracle cure." Any act that stems from a loving place can never be wrong even when the one you are extending love to, is you!

If we could hear the subconscious self-chatter of others around us, we would be nothing short of flabbergasted. How people treat and talk to themselves is not necessarily how they treat or talk to others. The same goes for you and me. On the outside we may show ourselves to friends and family as supportive, complimentary and loving, but then turn around and treat ourselves with judgment, unacceptance and scorn. Why is it that we hold others in such high regard but abuse the very person (self) who is most important? I stumbled upon the answer to this question during my awakening phase- The College of Kristen. It made so much sense and resonated so deeply in my soul, that it changed my perspective forever.

It has been said that when we are born, we come to this place as whole and complete units of our Divine Creator. Each and every one of us is an individual expression of the same Holy Love. There are no preconceived ideas, beliefs or philosophies in a newborn baby, only pure, unconditional Love. That's why babies are so untainted and unaffected in their first few years. They know nothing else but their Divinity. As we grow, we begin to hear the words spoken over us and around us through our parents, siblings, teachers, religions and society's rules and we start to form beliefs that there is something wrong with us. We are not yet conscious, strong or courageous enough to be able to separate out the Truth of Who we are against the opinions of others and we start to attach to and cultivate a subconscious belief of unworthiness. As time progresses, we may hear more polluted words and be the recipient of more hurtful behavior and sadly, these negative beliefs begin to solidify. By processing our life through a filthy filter of unworthiness, we can try and try to manifest our dreams, but never even get close. Unless or until we begin to undo our beliefs and truly grasp the understanding of our natural born worth, we will remain stuck. We will continue to deliver these false messages to ourselves and all we do in life will reflect those beliefs. Louise Hay states, *"If your mother did not know how to love herself, or your father did not know how to love himself, then it would be impossible for them to teach you to love yourself. They were doing the best they could with what they had been taught as children."* If we are conscious enough to take a wide open, objective look at our beliefs and patterns, we then actually have the chance to live the rest of our lives joyfully and authentically. The time has come to fully understand your worth and from this point forward, love yourself wholly and Holy to the absolute best of your ability.

Forgive Yourself

"It is very important for every human being to forgive herself or himself because if you live, you will make mistakes- it is inevitable. If we all hold on to the mistake, we can't see our own glory in the mirror because we have the mistake between our faces and the mirror; we can't see what we're capable of being. You can ask forgiveness of others, but in the end the real forgiveness is in one's own self."
–Maya Angelou

Once we truly begin to recognize our worth, we begin to understand that we are human, we are fallible and we are forgivable! Part of the pathway to empowerment, is to first understand our Divinity and then to forgive ourselves for any past mistakes that were expressions of our fearful, egoic and unworthy thinking. When we see ourselves as "bad", it is very difficult to navigate life in a productive, serving way. By learning to forgive ourselves quickly and treating ourselves with kindness and compassion, our soul awakens. We become more gentle with not only ourselves, but with our beloveds as well. We begin to lose attachment to "getting love" from the outside world for validation of our worth and we become more centered and peaceful. What happens is, **when we start to give ourselves the very things (love, compassion, kindness, forgiveness, acceptance) we have been seeking outside, our neediness begins to fall away and is replaced with a wonderful new self-image and confidence.** This then consecutively leads us to greater opportunities, greater adventures and greater people!

To further clarify egoic behavior and thinking, I am referring to the times when we behaved from our lower selves. The times we verbally attacked another, attempted to control another, stood in harsh judgment toward others or became overly passive, submissive or aggressive. I began to learn that any and all of this behavior stems from a tremendous lack of self-love - the shadows inside us that we have not yet healed. By not honoring our sacred selves, we don't stand in our natural grace and power as worthy individuals. I specifically recognized this in myself when someone would push one of my "unworthy buttons". I would become angry and would react or lash out in ways that did not demonstrate the love and kindness that was in my heart. This in turn would give others justified reason to say harsh things about me and again I would react. It was a vicious cycle. I just couldn't understand why no one could see me for Who I am. I eventually learned that it wasn't *others* who couldn't see me for Who I am, it was *I* who couldn't see me for Who I am. Inevitably, I would then guilt myself to death for my mistake and sink lower and lower and lower into the unworthiness abyss.

Let's say you do something that you feel very badly about and you can't seem to shake the guilt or shame associated with it. To hold onto those dense emotions is to put a heavy blanket (filter) on your personality and your life. How you show up in the world will be directly related to the shame and guilt filter you are now seeing yourself through. As Maya Angelou so beautifully stated at the head of this subchapter, "…the mistake stands between you and the mirror." If your mistake is not forgiven and dispelled, the next time you make a mistake, you will only add another blanket on top. It is somewhat easy to stand up and throw off one blanket, but can you imagine living under a lifetime of blankets (unforgiven mistakes)? That would be an awfully heavy burden to carry. When we forgive ourselves along the way, we keep our sacred self open and it is through an open-heart that we navigate our lives with empowerment.

My affirmation when I have made a mistake:
You did the very best you knew how at the time. You are human and you will make mistakes. I forgive you.
And then I go to God...
Holy Spirit, I am sorry for my mistake. My heart is open to your forgiveness. Please return me to my Right Mind so that I can move forward with peace and a better awareness of when I'm about to go wrong. Amen.

If you are one who does indeed have a lifetime of blankets piled on top of you, now is not the time to fret! *Reclaiming our personal power has no room for self-pity!* Start today. You were already forgiven by God when your mistake was made, now it is time to forgive *yourself.* As I began to forgive myself, I noticed how good I felt and I actually became excited to go back to mistakes of yesteryear and release myself from those prisons as well! It is like once I took the bold, first step, doors began to open, and open and OPEN! I was slowly being released from my own prison. Because of this process, my feelings around the mistakes became lighter and the mistakes morphed into mere memories rather than sources of shame.

Self-forgiveness *sets us free* by leaving behind the imprisonment of the past and aligning our minds and hearts for an empowering future. The freedom we gain from self-forgiveness is indescribably healing and has the capacity to shift our lives in glorious ways!

Four Steps to Self-Forgiveness and Release

1. **Understand your humanity**. You are not above, nor below anyone else. We are all equally fallible humans doing the very best we can. Your mistake, no matter how big or how small is not greater than or less than anyone else's. You are not bad, wrong or different from others because you have made a mistake. Understand your "oneness" with the rest of humanity in that you will make mistakes and they are forgivable.

2. **Recognize the value**. Recognize that through any forgiveness you are not condoning the mistake but releasing its power over your life. Understand that all mistakes are learning opportunities and set yourself free from the burden of it so that you may find the blessing

and move forward in life from a healthier perspective.

3. **Give it to God.** *A Course in Miracles* calls this The Atonement. It is the time where we recognize our wrong-mindedness (mistake) and give it to God. We hand our mistakes over to our Source, already knowing that we are fully forgiven and we pray for a change in perception. I have a visualization exercise where I imagine myself handing my mistake (or problem) over to *The Best Life Manager* (God) while standing in complete faith that I am fully protected and loved. In doing this, we are also aligning ourselves with Universal Intelligence so that we become co-creators of our experience. Through forgiveness, we keep our hearts open and an open heart is willing to receive.

4. **Let it be.** Once you have gone through the self-forgiveness process, it is simply time to just let... it... be. Surrender. To continue to revisit the mistake with shame or contempt is not forgiveness, but to reignite the power it has over you. To repeatedly relive it over and over again will only realign you with negative,

dense energy. Our job here is to rid ourselves of the unserving energy and cultivate a loving, forgiving and empowering awareness instead.

The 'How to' of Self-love

"Love yourself first and everything else falls into line. You really have to love yourself to get anything done in this world." –Lucille Ball

As with any conditioned mind patterns, one cannot break the cycle until she becomes highly aware of the pattern and then utilizes the necessary tools to make the changes. In this piece, I will demonstrate the processes I used to start loving myself. I made a dedication to my transformation, kept my focus on empowerment and soon thereafter, there was a *marked* alteration in my life. I was amazed to find how quickly my tools were working. Additionally, the peace and confidence I discovered created a passion in me to share it with the world. It was around this time I decided to write a book. I wanted to shout form the mountain tops, *"We don't have to suffer anymore! There is a way! And once we make the commitment, we must never give up!"*

I'd like to clarify that loving self is not about a warm, cuddly feeling when thinking about ourselves (although it's perfectly fine if it feels that way to you). Loving self is about the action(s) we take when our well-being is concerned. It is the commitment we make to ourselves to protect and nurture our sacred self as the worthy and important soul that we are.

In the list that follows, I name the tools and concepts I used to shift my overall perception of self and to cultivate a deep inner love.

1. **Stop looking outside for approval**. When you look to others for approval, you are giving another person your power. There is no one whose approval you need in order to express your authentic self. To seek outside is to negate all that you are. There is not another person on this planet who knows you the way you know yourself. Other people come equipped with opinions that are grown from their own fears, beliefs, ideas, passions and political status'. Others opinions of you will only be of approval if you are running congruent with their beliefs. There is simply no way to have everyone's

approval. Hence, what's true for you is the only thing that matters.

2. **Encourage your courage.** No great change can ever be made without courage. It will take courage to do almost anything substantial in life. Cultivating your courage and then taking steps forward is where the money is. Do not allow others' fears to hold you back. Look within and move in the direction of *your* dreams. Your courage will be a huge determining factor in how far you travel on this journey. As Maya Angelou once said, *"Courage is the most important of all the virtues because without courage, you can't practice any other virtue consistently."*

3. **Be compassionate to your experience.** Just as you would understand another's journey, understand and have compassion for yours. You know exactly what drives you or holds you back. Give yourself the safe place of compassion. Allow yourself to be exactly where you are without judgment. You have already committed to changing your life and you are working to change your position right now (that is why you are reading this book). Already, you have

shown great courage! To judge yourself harshly is to take several steps backward when you are working so hard to move forward.

4. **Forgive your fears.** As Marianne Williamson said, *"Love is what we we're born with. Fear is what we learned here."* Our fears have usually been fabricated from some experience of the past or the cunning workings of our ego (lower self) which does not want to see our growth. Although they may seem very real to you, all fear is an illusion. Again, to judge your fears is to cast dark energy in and around your growth and darkness only perpetuates fear. Fear can only be dispelled by Light. Forgiveness is Light. The egoic side of your human will **always** attempt to fear you out of forward movement. Be willing to face your fears, forgive your fears and move forward. Commit to a no-fear policy! (Within sound reason, of course!)

5. **Support yourself and honor your growth.** Each time I observed myself acting from a healthier place, I would *literally* pat myself on the back and say out loud, "Good job, Kristen!" I learned quickly how complimenting myself felt

incredible! It actually makes me smile out loud and my heart sing! Through this practice, the most amazing thing happened. I began to get stronger and stronger. The difference between outside and inside compliments is that when we support and congratulate ourselves, the compliment actually sticks and builds our self-esteem. Outside compliments may feel good at the moment, but they pass through us quickly, leaving us begging for more. *By supporting ourselves verbally and with deep authenticity, the need for outside validation will literally begin to fall away.* When we give ourselves unconditional love, we fill our hearts and when our heart is full, we will not *need* anything else.

6. **Respect your sacred self.** There is no person on this planet that is exempt from deserving respect and to withhold respect from yourself is to show other people that disrespectful treatment of you is okay. By learning to respect yourself, you are literally setting boundaries for others to follow. Respecting self consists of protecting yourself in all the ways you would protect a small child or loved one. If it's not acceptable for them, it is not

acceptable for you! Self-respect runs congruent with self-love. When we have one, we naturally have the other. All of these areas are intertwined in some way or form and it's up to us to treat ourselves the way we wish to be treated.

7. **Talk kindly to yourself.** The words we speak inward are the behaviors we show outward. When we are gentle with our inner-dialogue, we feel loved and supported and consequently we will behave in ways that support this. We cannot expect from others what we are not giving to ourselves. Speaking kindly to self, nurtures one's heart in ways that are indescribable, but become very obvious as one observes herself naturally beginning to show up differently in the world. Once this process gets underway, I can assure you, you will be very pleased with the results.

8. **Do not take things personally.** In Don Miguel Ruiz's book *The Four Agreements*, the one agreement that spoke the absolute loudest to me was *"Do Not Take Things Personally"*. Although I read that book long before my tsunami (and it rang bells then), I was put into a position to truly demonstrate this concept. By learning to

love myself, the need to take things personally naturally just fell away. This does not mean I am 100% great at this all the time! It does mean that a good 85-90% of the time, what others do or say about me does not illicit a strong emotional reaction anymore. Remember, what others say about us is not our business. What you say about you, *is* your business!

The road to empowerment rests on our willingness and commitment to self. When we truly understand our worth and make the necessary choices to facilitate our healing, a course is set that will lead us to reclaiming our personal power. We must become our own best friend and avid cheerleader. We must treat ourselves as the beautiful spirit and expression of God that we are. This is our birthright! Per the words of the beloved Bruce Lee, *"As we think, so shall we become."*

Thoughts to Ponder: *Am I gentle with myself? Do I forgive myself quickly for mistakes or do I relentlessly beat myself up? Do I treat myself differently than I do others? Do I honor the loving soul I am and encourage and support the true Essence of my being by demonstrating loving kindness with myself?*

Set the Intention: *I speak only loving and gentle words to myself. I am a beloved child of God and I am deserving of tender, compassionate words and supportive language. I forgive myself for my mistakes and I cherish my beautiful soul. And so it is.*

Chapter Three

Take Back Your Power -
You are Your Own Authority

"The ultimate authority must always rest with the individual's own reason and critical analysis."
–Dalai Lama

The life of a doormat is usually full of moments in time when we have allowed others to be the authority of what is right for us. Doormats tend to want to please others foremost to themselves and end up allowing others to be their authorities. We are currently seeking for approval/love and we falsely believe that we have to run everything we do by another to make it "okay". Healing this false belief is one the most important steps in reclaiming our personal power. This doesn't mean we cannot or should not run our ideas past our friends and family - I always believe in gathering opinions and information. **It means that when all opinions and information is gathered, we must then go within, discover what is right and true for ourselves and then make decisions that are most serving to our souls.** Giving others the power to make our decisions is like taking two steps forward and two steps back. We get nowhere fast. Additionally, we will find ourselves subconsciously fighting against our own inner knowing and become perplexed as to why we are struggling so desperately in our lives.

I remember when I first became a parent and I had to start disciplining my rambunctious two year old. My father was so enamored with her that every time I put her in time-out or disciplined her (which would make her cry), he would leave my house! He wouldn't say one word. I'd just come downstairs to find him gone even if he hadn't shared dinner with us which was why he was invited over in the first place. By not fully believing in the power of what I was doing, I would feel crushed that he was disapproving of my parenting and I began to withhold disciplining her in his presence. Inevitably, you can probably imagine what happened next. Over time, my toddler got out of control and I found myself even more upset and frustrated because now I had an unruly child! In my mind, I felt I couldn't find peace with either route I chose.

Eventually, I understood that I had to work past the feelings of the *perceived* disapproval and do what was right and serving for both me and my child. I must add that he never once spoke his disapproval to me. It was *I who assumed* what he was thinking. What came out much later was that due to his Grandpa soft-spot for her, he couldn't stand to hear her cry, so he removed himself from the situation. He admitted that how I was handling her was correct, but it was *he* that couldn't handle it. I didn't understand at that time that not only was I projecting my desperate need to please him outwardly, but I had completely misread a situation and made decisions based solely on another's approval. How I knew I should handle the situation - unruly child, discipline, hugs and kisses, happy baby, happy parent - became complicated and emotional solely because I was going against what I *instinctually* knew I should be doing.

Each and every one of us on this planet is equipped

with an inner knowing of what is right and true for ourselves. However, a pleasers need to be loved, approved of, seen, heard and/or acknowledged, will trump what we already know inside in order to gain what we are not giving ourselves. We create more chaos than needs be because we are not yet strong enough to stand behind our truths and inner knowing.

It's Between You and God

"When you have learned how to decide with God, all decisions become as easy and as right as breathing. There is no effort, and you will be led as gently as if you were being carried down a quiet path in summer."
– A Course in Miracles

Only you and the creative wisdom of Universal Intelligence can partner up in your life to bring about the best possible solutions to all that you face in your lifetime here on earth. Each and every person on this planet is a creation of the same Source Energy. Neale Donald Walsch creatively refers to each of us as "Deity Individuated". I fell in love with those words the minute I read them. Our connection to Source is what co-creatively works *with* us to manifest a life of abundance, love and joy. There is not one person on this planet who is an authority on what is best for you. They simply cannot be. Your journey, soul's calling and spiritual gifts are between you and God. No one else is equipped to reign over your life. It's just not possible.

Others may try to be your authority, but no matter how hard they try or how much they love you, they just simply do not have the power to tell you what is best for you. Your life is yours and you are the superlative judge of what is right and serving for you. Each one of us comes equipped with our very own inner guidance system (intuition) which is our connection to Source. It is through our logical thinking (left brain) and our Creative connection (right brain) that we are fully equipped to make great decisions that would best serve our soul and evolution. Problems arise when we lose the balance between the two. We can get stuck in one side of our brain and not allow the other to share in the decision making. Making good decisions for our lives requires an equal blend of logic, knowledge and analysis as well as gut instinct/intuition. Sometimes we may know what we need to do, but are not sure how to go about it. This is precisely when we need to gain more knowledge in the area (left brain) so we can plan a path. Other times we may logic our way through a situation and truly miss the deeper meaning behind things (right brain) because we are thinking way too hard to find an answer. This is precisely when we need to open up the energy center of our Creative Source (right brain) and allow for the flow of God's voice to come. Human beings are right and left brained for a reason. It is the most brilliant design. As Henri Bergson so beautifully stated, *"An absolute can only be given in an intuition, while all the rest has to do with analysis."*

More About Intuition

"The intuitive mind is a sacred gift and the rational mind is a faithful servant. We have created a society that honors the servant and has forgotten the gift. We will not solve the problems of the world from the same level of thinking we were at when we created them. More than anything else, this new century demands new thinking: We must change our materially based analyses of the world around us to include broader, more multidimensional perspectives."
–Albert Einstein

Miriam Webster dictionary describes intuition as: *The ability to understand something immediately, without the need for conscious reasoning.* Although we are all equally connected to Source, our connection is *unique* to our individual life and lessons required for our personal growth. We often *feel* (clairsentient), *see* (clairvoyant), *hear* (clairaudient) *or know* (claircognizant) this information through our intuition. When we begin to pay better attention to our intuition rather than the loud voices (ego/fear) in our heads and/or other people's opinions, we begin to forge a path of empowerment. It is through this connection that we strategize and act for our Highest Good. The more we do this, the better we feel about ourselves and our personal power begins to expand.

Our intuition is that clear, calm, quietly powerful voice inside us that leads us to the answers we are seeking. It is our powerful inner knowing, that instinctual pull, that leads us to manifesting our desires and best possible next step and/or solution to whatever it is we may be facing. Many people will say they do not receive intuitive "hits"; however, I beg to differ. There is no one who is exempt from this connection. The problem is they are just not quiet enough to hear it or they are unconscious to the messages coming. It has been said over and over throughout history, "my gut told me this, my heart told me that". This is what our inner voice is. It is intuition! It is Spirit moving through us, speaking to us and working with us. It is the voice that can lead us to greater things or forewarn us of impending dangers. It is a gentle, loving nudge in the right direction. As you may have noticed many times in crime solving shows, the detectives most often work from "hunches". There you go! It matters not what term is used to describe this inner knowing; only that one acknowledges and learns to trust in following it.

Many times in my life I have received a message and hit the DELETE button. Either I did not like what I was hearing or I discounted the message because it was not loud enough to drown out the cacophony of racket going on in my head (fear, overthinking). Each time I did not pay heed to my message, I found myself in a heap pile of mental chaos and suffering. Our messages are designed to help us, not hurt us. Spirit speaks to us in a loving, calm, quietly firm voice. They are simple, neutral-feeling messages that during our moments of peace can guide us to the next best step.

Before I even knew what intuition was I began to get

"hits" on people and situations. Learning to trust those messages and act accordingly is how we begin taking back our power. When I was about 9 years old, I *knew* (claircognizant) that a certain man was dangerous. I couldn't explain it to my mother other than, *"I just don't like him."* He was later convicted and imprisoned for pedophilia. My inner guidance at that tender age saved me from great harm. I didn't have the vocabulary to explain my feeling, but I trusted it completely. That is why I taught my children at a very young age to *feel* (while putting my hand over my heart) people. I would tell them if you *feel* someone is not safe, no matter who the person is chances are he/she is not safe! When I was approximately 37 years old, I repeatedly *heard* (clairaudient) over a six week period of time, *"a sister is going to die."* Six weeks later, I lost a dear friend and her daughter to a drunk driver. It was a terribly sad and tragic blow to us all.

Although the examples I shared here are major life upsets, our intuition can readily guide us in our day to day "normal" decisions such as where to purchase a new home or where to find a comfortable pair of shoes for work. Spirit is *always* with us because we are One. There simply is no separation. When we begin to fine tune our connection, we begin to fine tune our lives. Our life begins to flow easier and we make fewer decisions that we regret later on.

What is True for You?

"It is very easy to conform to what your society or your parents and teachers tell you. This is a safe and easy way of existing; but that is not living… To live is to find out for yourself what is true." –Jiddu Krishnamurti

Most of us in childhood are constantly told what is best for us physically, emotionally, morally and religiously. We look upon our parents, teachers, elder siblings, family members and religious figures as the almighty great ones who know all. We may have even seen them as faultless and perfect. For the most part, it didn't even occur to us to question their authority and we blindly followed where they led. I know I certainly did. I felt as though my mother could do no wrong, my older brothers were gods and my assigned religion was the only map for my life. If I was told I was a brat, stupid, going to hell, weird, a sinner etc. I believed it and if they told me to jump, I did. As the years approached somewhere around junior high I began to question everything. I started to see people as fallible humans rather than perfect and all knowing. I discerned that everyone was learning just as I was. (Although I didn't understand the magnitude of this concept at the time) Some of the conditioned mind still had a hold on me, but some things just DID NOT FEEL RIGHT to me any longer. That was when I left my assigned religion and set out on my own spiritual path and quest for Truth. By 20 years old, when asked what church I attended, I replied, *"The Church of Kristen."* I decided that *I* was going to decide what felt right and true for myself.

As my path unraveled before me and life continued to happen, I became closer and closer to what was real and true for me. I began to see the world through a whole new kaleidoscope of colors and additionally, I began to recognize more fully the inner voice that was always within me, guiding me. I may have left an organized religion but I never left or doubted my Higher Power. On this quest for Self and Truth, I learned a great deal. I don't want it assumed this all came at once in one huge awakening. I am speaking here about process and the allowance of an open heart and mind for knowledge and wisdom to come. I'd like to disclaim that I am not judging or calling anyone's parents, family members or religions wrong or bad. I am saying that we do not have to jump on the bandwagon of what *others'* think is best for us. Once we hit adulthood, we are free to live, be and do as we like in the ways that are most serving to our souls and higher selves. How others perceive life and how *they choose* to live, does not have to be your gospel.

Returning to Center and Presence

> *"We are here to awaken from our illusion of separateness."* –Thich Nhat Hanh

> *"Life is only available in the present moment."*
> -Thich Nhat Hanh

There will be moments in our life when we get so wrapped up in the physical plane of life - job, kids, money, career - that we forget Who we are. We will feel disconnected from Source (although we never are) and perhaps feel a sense of floundering about, un-fulfillment, lack of ambition and passion or that life is simply meaningless and difficult. It is important during these times to recognize that we are careening out of control and then reroute ourselves in order to return to center. We are not doing ourselves any favors running around stressed or non-present. If anything, we are doing ourselves a grave disservice. In those moments, due to lack of faith and strength, we run the risk of taking another's words as gospel and acting according to his or her idea of what is right and true only to later discover we made a terrible choice. By simply becoming *aware* that we are not in a good position to be making decisions, we can refrain until we are have more clarity. My favorite prayer during these moments is:

> *God, I am aware that I am confused. Please help the right information find me so that I can make a great decision here. Amen.* (And then I surrender)

Once the emotional upheaval has been recognized, we are now able to carve out some quiet time, say a prayer and become fully present while our next best step is known.

There is no authority over our journey other than ourselves. Having a rooted, deep connection with Source is the best way to locate and enhance this power. I often say to clients who are lost or wishy-washy in decision making, "You already *know* what you need to do. It's time to get quiet around this situation and let your answers come to you… because when you ask the Universe for answers, they *will* come." Nine times out of ten the client will reply, "Yes… I do already know…" God's communication with us cannot be heard through the cacophony of chatter in our minds. With all that racket going on, we can usually only hear the loudest voice (the shouting ego) and the voice of Spirit becomes difficult to discern.

Finding time to reconnect to yourself and God is the place where miracles happen. It is in this place of quiet that we hear the messages, changes in perception and answers being sent our way. What this means is, anytime we can slow down and clear our minds, we have provided a landing strip for the messages to arrive. This is why I dedicated a chapter in this book to meditation and contemplation. A quiet mind is imperative when listening for our guidance. A daily morning and evening meditation practice helps facilitate peace throughout our day because we tend to be able to return to center more readily. Remember, there is not much guidance being received while we are marathoning our way through life. A lot is lost if we don't become aware enough to s l o w d o w n and allow for the graceful unfolding.

Manipulation Strategies of Others

"Your time is limited, so don't waste it living someone else's life. Don't be trapped by dogma - which is living with the results of other people's thinking. Don't let the noise of others' opinions drown out your own inner voice. And most important, have the courage to follow your heart and intuition." –Steve Jobs

Challenges arise when we allow others to tell us what we need to do, when to do it or how to do it. Oftentimes what others are telling us to do is aimed at making themselves comfortable and is not truly for *our* Highest Good. It is their attempt to control our lives in order to make themselves feel safe/comfortable/happy. For example: You may be desiring to make a switch from a corporate, desk job to something that is more creative and passion-filled such as painting murals. Your father may tell you it's a bad idea and it would be in your best interest to stay put. *Your* "secure" job makes *him* feel safe! He enjoys the fact that you are gainfully employed, that you have insurance and 401k benefits and the idea of you starting your own business from the ground up, scares the heck out of him. He may even attempt a good round of fear, guilt and/or manipulation to get the job done. What can happen next if we are not dialed into this type of behavior is that their fear may then activate our fears and then we allow our fear to take root eventually sabotaging our soul's desires. Where we sought for outside validation, we got fear instead. Where we looked to be validated, we were squelched. This dynamic is very common for a person who is attempting to build strength. *We can mistakenly allow others' fears to exemplify our own or even become our own.* When this happens we tend to ignore our inner urges and desires and eventually our dreams begin to deflate. Soon enough we default back to our safety zone with nothing gained.

In finding the courage to stand in your power, it is important to know and remember that your journey, personal experiences and lessons are yours and yours alone. No two journeys are alike no matter how similar they may appear. Others may give us advice (whether we seek it or not) and it is up to us to discern whether their words resonate within or not. Many people walk this earth shrouded in a blanket of fear and they attempt to control their world (and you may be in that world) in order to feel secure. They may have made a mistake in their past and desperately want to stop you from making the same one. What they do not understand, is that you are walking your own path, and although things might appear similar, no two paths are alike. At the end of the day, you are simply gathering information in order to choose wisely for yourself.

By becoming *consciously aware* of such things, you have already passed through a barrier and have taken a mighty leap toward empowerment. Awareness is key to almost anything in life. What we are aware of, we are able to work with.

An empowered person allows others to state their opinion, because knowledge and wisdom are powerful; however, when decision making time arrives, an empowered individual does what feels right and true to her.

I invite you today to give yourself permission to have your very own beliefs and thought systems. You are an authentically unique individual and it is important to truly know and own that fact on the road to recovery. It is your time to live from you own Truth and create a uniquely beautiful life that fulfills YOU. We are not here on earth to prove anything to anyone or to live a life that another chooses for us. We are here on earth as Spirit having a human experience. It is important to understand that *your* path and *your* spiritual gifts are uniquely and beautifully yours to develop, experience and celebrate!

Trust Yourself

"As soon as you trust yourself, you will know how to live." – Johann Wolfgang von Goethe

For some, trusting themselves is tricky. They may believe they did not make good decisions in the past so they no longer trust themselves and they look to others to help them make better decisions. They also may allow others to make their decisions so that they are not to "blame" if things goes awry. If you are truly serious about making the transition from doormat to empowerment, it is paramount to begin making your own decisions. It may feel difficult at first to trust yourself and your inner knowing about what is true and right for you, but it is *the only way* to live the life you have always wanted. You may make a few mistakes along the way and that is perfectly okay. We all make mistakes while we are learning. A virtuoso was once a beginner. It's the sheer willingness to *become* something better that drives us to success.

It's important to say that it is perfectly fine to discuss options with your support system as long as the final decision is yours. In decision making, it is your intellect, coupled with Source's guidance and love that will lead you down the correct path. How many times have you said, *"I should have done it the other way. I* **knew** *it and I chose to ignore it!"?* What you were led to do *initially* is your guidance system co-creating with you. That is the place where all final decisions should come from. To listen to anyone/anything outside of your own intuition and knowledge will only sabotage your spiritual evolution and your life.

We all have intuitive whispers telling us the best choice, but we are so clouded with fear and over thinking, that we oftentimes take the safest route. But does that "safe route" necessarily guarantee our happiness? It does not. We usually gain the opposite-the pain of an unfulfilled life. It takes courage and faith in self to listen and step into our own light to create a new life. If you are unsure as to what you want to do at the moment, do nothing. Sometimes the gap between answers is where we become secure with our upcoming decision because in that gap, we will receive many signs leading us in one direction or another. When we do finally decide which direction to go, we will feel at peace with our decision.

On the road to empowerment, it is very important to stop giving away your decision making authority and power. Have compassion and love for those who are trying to "help" you, but indisputably know that you are your own best authority. Be grateful for the people around you who believe they know what is best for you and be willing to smile and say, "Thank you. I got this."

Thoughts to Ponder: *Do I allow others to tell me how to live my life? Do I allow others' opinions regarding my life overrule my own opinion or make me over-question my choices? Do I trust the inner guidance coming to me?*

Set the Intention: *This is my life and I am the only authority over what is right and true for me. I trust in my ability to make clear and knowledgeable decisions that are right and serving to my soul and personal journey. And so it is.*

Chapter Four

Authenticity -
Where True Connection Begins

"Always be yourself, express yourself, have faith in yourself, do not go out and look for a successful personality and duplicate it." –Bruce Lee

Being authentic in your life means being bold enough to be who you truly are. It's about embracing every nuance, quirk, talent, expression of love, passionate belief and humor along with multitudes of other things that make you *uniquely you*. It's about standing up bravely in expression of who you are no matter what reactions or prejudices come from others. It is about letting go of outcomes and/or trying to be something you are not for the sake of pleasing someone else. It's absolute, true honesty with self and others even if your choices may disappoint another or separate you from the crowd. *Being authentic is the giving of unconditional love and acceptance to oneself.* By knowing we are enough, we find the courage to be authentic. It's about honoring ourselves from the same level as our Divine Creator honors us.

You need YOU. Your children and loved ones need YOU. The world needs YOU. There is no other person on this planet that possesses the exact qualities as you. So often we travel through life insecure with our genuine nature because it doesn't fit in with who *we think we should be* in order to blend with the world. And by the way, who ever said that we have to blend with the world to be successful and knew what they were talking about? No one ever. In fact, the most famous inventors, revolutionaries, artists, visionaries, musicians and spiritual teachers were not interested in blending with anything. They took what was deep inside their souls and had the courage to share it with the world. They were not concerned with being laughed at or not fitting in. They took what was authentically true for them and worked towards living a life that reflected their truths.

When we commit to owning, celebrating and displaying our genuine authentic selves, our life begins to open up and evolve in unimaginable ways. We start to attract people and circumstances that support our authenticity and we invite the Universe to work *with* us to create a life that is custom designed to fulfill us in the most deep and organic way. We release the need to be perfect and we absolve ourselves from the opinions of others that have kept us imprisoned for so long. We no longer live outside our true nature and the heavy burden of living up to a perceived standard is lifted off our shoulders. We watch as the dynamics of our relationships change from superficial and fearful to genuine and safe and we bask in that joy. When we learn to be who we are without apology, we become free.

Getting to Know the REAL You

"The privilege of a lifetime is to become who you truly are." - C.G. Jung

"To find yourself, think for yourself." – Socrates

By finally admitting that we haven't truly been 100% authentic in our lives, we have given rise to finally discovering our complete selves. When we know ourselves completely, we are more likely to honor that self and not get caught up in the hysteria of the crowd mentality. If we don't get to know ourselves well, we will be wishy-washy in our morals and values and end up making terrible decisions. Like Aaron Tippin states in his country song, *"You've got to stand for something or you'll fall for anything. You've got to be your own man [woman] not a puppet on a string."* By getting magnificently clear on Who we are and what we stand for, we raise the odds exponentially of living a life that honors our passions, dreams and goals. **Others will not honor us if we don't first honor ourselves and the Universe cannot assist us in creating a wonderful life if we are not first assisting ourselves.**

How well we know ourselves, is proportional to how well others can know us. When we are exceptionally clear about Who we are and what we stand for, we are able to deliver this message directly and indirectly into the world. Directly through our actions and words and indirectly through the energy we resonate out into the cosmos. Through authenticity, we organically begin to attract people, situations, relationships and jobs that match our vibrational frequency and are better suited for us.

Hidden within the following questions are aspects of one's genuine nature. We can learn so much about ourselves by asking ourselves powerful questions and being daringly honest. Be mindful that these answers are about you and only you. Do your best to refrain from processing through the filter of what someone else would want from you. I invite you to write them down on paper, own your truths and make them real by forging a hard copy that you can refer to or add to at any time.

Who is the REAL me?

1. *Where or how do I like to spend my leisure time?*
2. *How do I feel about God and religion?*
3. *What are my desires, passions and interests? What ignites my inner fire?*
4. *What are my morals and highest values?*
5. *What are my future goals?*
6. *What is my ideal relationship partner?*
7. *What types of people do I like to be around and have as friends?*

8. *What time do I like to go to bed and rise in the morning?*

9. *What does a perfect day look like to me and how can I achieve more of that in my life?*

10. *What aspects of my life/beliefs am I not willing to compromise for another?*

11. *What keeps me well balanced and centered?*

Now, how did that feel? I can bet it felt pretty darn good to go within and honor yourself! Now take some time to breathe into these truths and allow them to settle into every cell of your body. Own them. Celebrate them. Love them. This is who you are and what needs to be honored in order to live a fully empowered life. Without acknowledging and standing behind our truths, we cannot possibly manifest a life that fulfills our soul's calling.

Love and Honor Your Authentic Self

"The light that will come forth from within you will help you heal yourself and all those who come into your presence. The world needs you." –Debbie Ford

"When you are content to be simply yourself and don't compare or compete, everybody will respect you."
–Lao Tzu

A doormat can spend her whole life answering to the wants of others and constantly forsaking her own life's purpose and joy in exchange. The truth is, the doormat may do this to please others or to feel momentarily loved by others, but when we are constantly striving to please others at the expense of ourselves, we are not loving nor honoring ourselves. Once again we are seeking "outside" for what we already have "inside". Additionally, we are enabling stagnation in our relationships instead of serving as a vessel for evolution, because others cannot grow within an inauthentic environment either. Sometimes the word 'no', a genuine answer based on your own best interest or your insight and/or ideas is exactly what the relationship needs to uncover areas that may need healing or change.

Being authentic is about claiming who you are for all of your personal, unique magnificence. People may still try to change you to make themselves more comfortable, but the more secure you are about who you are, the less likely you can or will be manipulated or controlled. One of my favorite mentors, Dr. John Demartini, states, *"Wherever we don't empower ourselves in our lives, someone will overpower."* Don't be willing to sacrifice your authenticity, heart, soul or goals for another. Tap into your true self and what it is that makes you happy and ignites your inner fire. Over the years, many people have said to me, "But I don't know who I am!" My answer to that always is, "You just are!" It's not about trying to find some secret passcode to unlock yourself or to consciously design a fascinating person to wow! the world with. It's truly about honoring that self you already are - the way you were designed. No one on this planet is exempt from brilliance or amazing qualities, ideas, opinions or passions. Who you are and what you can contribute to the collective whole of life is greater than you could ever imagine! You don't have to win the Pulitzer Prize or write dozens of best sellers to contribute to the greater good of the planet. Simply by **being you**, an individual aspect of God, you have the ability to inspire, heal and bring joy to many others. Your words, ideas and wisdom are beautiful fragments of our Divine Creator that can set forth tremendous healing for not only one individual, but it will produce a ripple effect that may actually serve the entire world.

Sounds fantastical, but it is true! However, this cannot be done if you are playing small and flying under the radar of your genuine nature. If you truly wish for the healing and joy that comes as expressions of living authentically, it's time to get real about Who you are and start living in that place every day.

Why a 'False Self' Works Against Us

"No one man can, for any considerable time, wear one face to himself, and another to the multitude, without finally getting bewildered as to which is the true one."
– Nathaniel Hawthorne

Have you ever been around someone who "sold" themselves to you as something they were not? For example: Perhaps a partner initially fawned all over you and was concerned with your every comfort. You might have been thinking, *"Wow, this is so great! I really, really matter to this guy!"* - only to discover after he captured his prey, he really didn't give a darn about your comfort and well-being and really only cared about his own. How did you feel when you discovered the real person? Did you feel betrayed? Were you incredibly disappointed? Did you wonder if the connection you thought you had was even real? My guess is you probably did. When a person is desperate for love and attention, they can oftentimes mold themselves into any character they think will gain the approval of others. They can be so good at the game, that you may not even know who they truly are for a very long time. I call these people con-artists. Whether a con-artist is exploiting money from vulnerable people or exploiting love and attention from you, it's still a con. It's important to know that this concept can also be reciprocally true. If *we* are not showing up authentically, *we* run the risk of selling a false bill of goods to another and then *we* become the con-artist.

The truth is, sometimes we may not even know we are doing it. We may have been living behind a mask for so long, that it gets difficult to differentiate between what is real and what is not. Our personality becomes that of "follower" and "pleaser" and we lose track of the true nature of our essence and personalities. However, I'm going to cut us all a break right here… Most often, this behavior came into place as a protection mechanism that has become our unconscious conditioned way of being. It is a fabrication of our lower selves that believed the judgments spoken over us in our pasts.

We falsely learned that who we genuinely are, is not good enough. So with that, breathe a sigh a relief and know we have all done it and it holds no bearing to how splendid any one of us really is! The time is now to open your mind to a new and better way to be so you can put an end to the fearful, protective cage that has kept you jailed for far too long.

My client, Lindsay, was nearing her 40's. She was starting to feel desperate about meeting a man and getting married. Every time we spoke, she changed her idea on what kind of man she wanted to date. She constantly changed her values based on what she *assumed* her current potential partner would want. For one thing, she constantly went back and forth on the topic of children - yes, he can have them, no, he cannot, yes, she wants her own, no, she does not. She was so confused as to what she really wanted because she was too busy keeping up with whatever she *assumed* her potential partner wanted. If she thought he wanted a party girl, she became that. If she thought he wanted an intellectual girl, she became that. Eventually the true nature of Lindsay would come through and the man she was dating would begin to notice that she was not inherently the person she displayed herself to be.

He would sense her dependency and weakness and consequently, the relationship would begin to crumble and eventually end in pain.

In conjunction with this, subconsciously Lindsay would doubt the man's affections and would become very insecure within the relationship thus causing even more upheaval. She doubted his love because *she was not being real.* Subconsciously she knew she was not living within her authentic nature and her partner was falling for an imposter. Her inner psyche would always question his attraction. Unless or until Lindsay can learn to love herself and show up in the world as the true unique, awesome human being she is, she will continue to repeat this pattern.

The same type of thing can happen in our day to day life. If we are not portraying who we truly are, we cannot receive the love, support and compassion that can connect us to our friends and family even better. We tend to float through life believing we can do it all ourselves. One of my difficult areas was being able to show hurt feelings. I grew up in a household of boys and if I cried, they'd get in trouble with the parents and upset with me. Hence, I stopped crying altogether and concocted the belief that: *when I am genuine with my feelings and thoughts, I upset others and lose their love and attention.* Through conditioning, showing my hurt feelings meant I was annoying and needy. This belief was the core reason why I began withholding feelings of emotional pain or sadness. I wanted to prove to my brothers and the world that I wasn't annoying or needy. My false persona was so good, that as I grew, others wouldn't notice when I truly was in pain and when asked, I'd tell everyone I was fine. Consequently, I'd harbor resentment and anger because *"no one cared about me or was helping me!"* and when I couldn't hold it in any longer and finally did speak up, it came out toxic and spiteful. Little did I know I was not portraying to the world a girl who was in pain. No one had any clue that all I really needed was a little love and compassion.

Learning to share my feelings gently as they arose and asking for help, not only made for a happier me, but it gave others the opportunity to give their love to me. Not only did I get the help I needed, my friends and loved ones got the opportunity to be in service which made them feel great as well. Additionally, my authenticity and vulnerability allowed us to connect on a deeper, more intimate level and our relationship(s) became stronger. Both sides can and do win on some level when we are courageous enough to portray our genuine selves.

How Authentic *are* You?

> *"This above all:*
> *To thine own self be true,*
> *And it must follow, as the night the day,*
> *Thou canst not then be false to any man."*
> – Hamlet, Shakespeare

In retrospect of my life, I always thought I was living it in the fullest expression of my true nature. During my College of Kristen, I soon uncovered several areas where I was holding myself back. I'll admit, I was quite astounded when I discovered this because I've always been an open book. I truly felt I was *always* genuine. Learning that this was untrue had such a huge impact on me that it became one of the chapters of this book. I uncovered areas where I would withhold my truth to minimize confrontation, for fear of not wanting to offend another or for fear of judgment and non-acceptance. If someone gossiped about another person, I would join in even if I disagreed or knew it was wrong. If everyone was having an alcoholic beverage, I had one too even if I really had no interest in drinking that night. I learned (the hard way) how withholding my truth was causing my self-esteem to deplete because I was not honoring my authentic self. I didn't like me, so I couldn't believe others did. This new awareness spawned a new commitment to always live my life in alignment with my truth. My new plan ended up playing a monumental part in my pathway to empowerment. It took time, practice and a whole lot of courage, but the powerful shift that came from it was well worth it.

Now is the time to get down to uncovering how authentic you have been living up until now by asking yourself the following questions. This exercise is designed to bring any lies or false beliefs to the forefront so they may be transcended. I invite you to allow for extreme honesty.

How Authentic are You Really?

1. *Do I do what I **truly** want/feel/believe or do I acquiesce to others' ideas and opinions because it is easier or because I don't want to be judged or shamed?*
2. *Do I allow others to make decisions for me?*

3. *How often in my life do I put my wants/desires on hold for another?*

4. *Do I make decisions out of love of self or to please another?*

5. *Am I being true to myself and allowing the whole of me to show?*

6. *Am I open with my fears and allow my emotions to show?*

7. *Do I hide under the guise of "I'm a patient person" when another's behavior is unacceptable in order to avoid conflict or the unknown?*

I imagine that solely based on the fact that you are reading a book on doormat recovery, the above questions most likely revealed a few areas where you haven't been demonstrating your true self. Now is not the time to fret. It's the time to celebrate because you have just moved a little closer to your empowerment! It has been said by several of my clients, that the concept of authenticity and vulnerability was *the key* to unlocking the life they always dreamed of. They shared how it was the missing ingredient to their lives and it all began by becoming aware of the places they were withholding their true selves. They no longer assume that another person already knows what they need, want or feel. Through this, they have gained a better understanding of not only themselves, but of their loved ones as well. By allowing themselves to be vulnerable, wonderfully clarifying and healing dialogues ensued that were sorely missing before. They began to notice how the love bonds strengthened in their relationships and their self-esteems expanded when their genuine nature was not only accepted, but celebrated!

Release the Need for Approval

"If I had a prayer, it would be this: 'God spare me from the desire for love, approval, and appreciation. Amen.'"
–Byron Katie

Historically being a life-long seeker of love outside of myself, I knew no other way than to try to please others. I subconsciously felt that if I catered to others' needs and wants, and adjusted my personality accordingly, I was sure to get the approval I was craving so much. It didn't work. Little did I know that the approval (love) I was craving so badly was my own and by constantly bending and flexing for others I was not loving myself. When we look outside ourselves for love and attention, our *need* becomes a bottomless pit. This need acts much like a hungry beast with an insatiable appetite. When we constantly do for others rather than taking care of self, we actually perpetuate this inner hunger and act in ways that do not uphold our highest values or serve our best interests. We are acting inauthentically out of fear instead of acting authentically out of love and acceptance of self. We can become exhausted, unmotivated and oftentimes depressed.

During my College of Kristen, I consciously removed things from my life (dating, going out a lot, television) that would serve as distractions from my healing. I spent a lot of time getting quiet and going within. I focused on *being* rather than *doing*. The byproduct of not trying to **be** or **do**, allowed me to discover something… Me. I slowly began to embrace who/what my soul was calling me to be. Over time, I became so organically myself that if/when I attempted to live outside my authenticity, I became very uncomfortable. This was my new truth. I learned to express what honored my soul even if I thought it wouldn't get the popular vote. I began to do things that inspired me and brought me joy and excitement no matter what anyone thought about it. I learned about setting loving boundaries and not feeling guilty afterward. I discovered my inner brilliance and began to trust what I found. It's not enough to just explore your genuine self, you must be willing to grasp onto it and put it into action. This is self-love! This is releasing the need for others' approval.

"Truly being authentic is knowing what matters to you, on the deepest level of who you are, and committing always to act from that authentic center."
– Richie Norton

Being authentic is about giving yourself permission to matter and not being sorry that you do. For example, if my friends invite me to something that I am simply not interested in, I say no. I no longer worry about the possibility that they might get upset with me or may not like me anymore. I stay true to myself unapologetically. I don't do things anymore just to "fit in." If they later decide not to invite me anymore because I do not fall into the mold of their values, then I view it as perfect. If a space is created in my life by losing a couple of people, there is now space to fill with people who are a better vibrational fit for me. If my friends decide to honor my position and love me anyway, I have discovered their true character as well. I don't fret that I will not have any friends because I know the Universe abhors a vacuum. When there is space in our life for creation, you better bet the Universe will work with you to fill the space with something for your highest good. Our job is to stay true to ourselves, practice patience and allow the Universe to work its magic. Being open to the flow of life is *pertinent* in the implementation of living our authentic lives. Letting go of control and *allowing,* is when things begin to fall into place naturally through our deep connection to self. It is about being able to say *this* is what I believe, *this* is what I like and *this* is Who I am without fear.

Note: It's important to mention that being unapologetically you *does not* give us license to excuse our crappy behavior. Being rude, mean, abusive, a name-caller, manipulative or controlling does not get excused because we claim it's our genuine nature. To do this is a profound misuse of energy and it will not get you the results you are seeking. We must stay mindful and highly conscious as to what we claim as our genuine nature. This book and this work are solely spotlighting the areas one needs to heal and transcend in order to achieve personal empowerment.

* * *

To be authentic is to dress how you want to dress, to say what you want to say, to do the activities that bring *you* joy and the giving of authentic 'no's' and 'yes's''. **It is living in balance with one's own needs as well as the needs of our loved ones.** It is to step up and live our true uniqueness for all that we are. When we finally discover, accept and own all of Who we are, without the need for approval, we become inspired. Our inner fire ignites! Our life comes alive as if it was repainted with new vibrant colors. We begin to draw people to us who are attracted to our Divine Essence and we can then have faith in knowing that the people choosing to spend time with us really enjoy our company and not that of a false persona we concocted. In living a life of love and respect of self, we will attract reciprocal energy through a direct and indirect shift in our vibration. When our vibration rises, our relationship to everything rises. Life begins to present new and exciting people and opportunities to us. A happier you, becomes a happier parent, lover, friend and co-worker. We no longer flounder about choices or are easily swayed by what others perceive as valuable - but only by what we perceive as valuable. When we put our fears of acceptance and approval aside to live within our truth… shift happens!

"Sincerity is the fulfillment of our own nature, and to arrive at it we need only follow our own true Self. Sincerity is the beginning and end of existence; without it, nothing can endure." –Tzu-ssu

Thoughts to Ponder: *What is it that I want for myself, my life? What expressions of me have I been suppressing in order to gain acceptance? Am I willing to start showing my uniqueness to the world?*

Set the Intention: *I am safe in expressing my true self. I am whole and perfect just the way I am. The world needs my gifts and talents. I am willing to step into my authenticity and create the life I desire. And so it is.*

Chapter Five

Building a Supportive Community - Understanding Your Tribe

"Encourage, lift and strengthen one another. For the positive energy spread to one will be felt by us all. For we are connected, one and all." -Deborah Day

When we begin the journey to empowerment, we can feel quite unsteady and very afraid. In this new phase of growth, we have not yet realized our full worth, potential or strength, and oftentimes we question everything we are doing: *Is this okay? Am I doing the right thing? What if? What if? What if?* Our lack of confidence can make us easy prey to the negative messages and/ or judgments of others. The fear others are holding in their hearts can amplify the fear we are holding in our own, and darken the little bits of light we are just beginning to see. It's important to recognize we are in a tricky and uncomfortable place and to allow "Negative Nellies" and naysayers into our minds will only impede our growth. Personal transformation can shake up a lot fear and having loving, positive support can actually aid in facilitating our growth and keep us on track. It is essential right now and from this point forward, that we are careful about the people we use as our sounding boards, and equally important, the media we choose to fill our minds with.

The word "community" in this chapter, references the people whom we share ourselves with physically and emotionally as well as the external stimuli we allow into our lives. It embodies the people we turn to when our struggles get the best of us and the resources we use to keep us inspired and in alignment with our evolution. Our best community is a tribe of individuals and media resources, who are like-minded and growth oriented and will uplift, inspire and motivate us daily to keep moving forward when we feel like quitting. Aside from our friends and family, our tribe can include: uplifting social media sites, spiritual and self-help programs and communities, support groups or seminars, and/or a wide range of inspirational literature.

Our community should serve as the figurative hand that lifts us up when we have stumbled and/or the reassuring pat on the butt to get back in the game when we feel exhausted or defeated. It's about surrounding ourselves with daily inspiration that will lovingly remind us of Who we are when we have forgotten and individuals who are courageous enough to tell us the hard truths when we may be stuck believing our own lies. When we feel safe within another's company and we truly know they have our best interests at heart, we are aligning ourselves for solutions and victory. We are with our mighty companions.

Periodic Maintenance Checks

"You cannot hang out with negative people and expect to live a positive life." - Joel Osteen

Prior to my tsunami, I had never before realized just how sensitive I was to the verbal and nonverbal messages I was getting from other people through their reactions/responses to our conversations. I began to take keen notice how spending time with one person felt very different than spending time with another. I also noticed how certain media had the same effect on me. I had allowed others' perspectives to breed fear within me. The negativity they were spewing, only served to reinforce my negativity and even create some where there wasn't any! As I progressed through my College of Kristen, I began to take note of the people in my life who seemed to truly care about me and were eager to help me transcend my current hell. Consecutively, I also began to take note of the Negative Nellies who lived beneath a dark cloud and were only interested in perpetuating my current pain. Interestingly, the common denominator I discovered with the Negative Nellies was they were the ones who were the most unhappy, unmotivated and anxious in *their own lives.* I realized that prior to this new awareness, I had been seeking help from people who were not empowered within their own lives and people cannot share or give what they do not possess themselves. That doesn't make them bad or wrong; it only means I was looking for hope and encouragement in all the wrong places!

The key to knowing if your present community is beneficial for you is, to periodically perform maintenance checks. Below is a short list of questions you may ask yourself to check the status of your current community.

- Does my community/friend help me feel like my situations are conquerable or do they aid in perpetuating my fear?
- Does my community challenge me in my thoughts and beliefs or do they just agree with whatever stance I am taking?
- Do I feel judged while I share my life situations or do I feel accepted and loved?
- Are my confidants positive and empowered or defeated victims of life?

The answers to these questions can be the guidance you need while determining if your current community is serving your highest good. As with all empowerment work, it is very important to be completely honest with your answers. We cannot move forward without complete personal integrity. Even if you cringe at what you are revealing, it is still vitally important to at least recognize it even if you are unwilling *at this moment* to make a change. Mere recognition (without action), is still growth.

We don't necessarily have to demolish our existing

community in order to bring in additional members, although in some cases, that might be necessary. In most cases, a bit of a "light remodeling" is what's required. It's more about being fully aware of who you surround yourself with and what information/opinions you are taking in. Like a person wanting to lose weight has to watch what she puts into her mouth, a recovering doormat has to be aware of who she shares space with. Having a solid set of empowering friends around us is like providing the best nutrients to our soil in order for our healing garden to grow.

Shortly into my tsunami, I began to notice how others were reacting to my situation and to me. There were the ones who angrily added to my drama, the ones who simply didn't give a crap and the ones who figuratively held me in their arms as I shared my pain and confusion - their dialogue always filling me with hope and inspiration. Something inside of me woke up. From that moment on, I began to be very aware of who I went to for guidance and support. I now fully understood how important one's community of friends and confidantes really is and about one year into the College of Kristen, I repeated this powerful intention several times a day:

I attract only people of good character and integrity.
I am open to receiving an abundance of solid
friendships in my life. I attract people who care
about my well-being as much as I care about theirs.
I am grateful for the amazing friendships I have.
And so it is.

Almost immediately, the disrespectful, negative and harmful people in my life began to fall away and new, light-filled people of good integrity began to fall in! The most amazing part was that I began to see this happen very soon after setting my intention. I already had a few awesome members of my circle; however, I went on to meet several more. Nothing I ever said or did made this powerful, loving community cringe or want to run away. They loved me no matter what mood or struggle I was experiencing at the time. This reconstruction proved to enhance my growth/healing in ways that I could never have imagined. I now had a mighty community of friends who were as willing to assist me in my growth, as I was in theirs. Through their space holding and love, I began to heal more quickly than if I had had to do it alone. The American poet and academic Haniel Long once said, *"Each of us is a being in himself and a being in society, each of us needs to understand himself and understand others, take care of others and be taken care of himself."*

Tune Out the Naysayers

"First they ignore you. Then they laugh at you. Then they fight you. Then you win." -Mohandas Gandhi

Let it be known, it is not impossible to grow within an already existing community, even if it is a non-supportive one, because personal growth and awareness is inevitably *always our choice.* However, it can be extremely difficult to lift oneself out of uncertainty and fear when others are fueling our fires. What Gandhi so succinctly states above is that, it is most important to know *your* truth, know what is right for you and then be willing to stand behind your truth no matter what resistance you come up against. Our souls are always leading us - this is *our truth.* Our truth may not be congruent with another's opinion; however, that has no bearing on the importance of it. How easily we are able to stand in our truth always comes in direct proportion to our level of self-esteem. And our level of self-esteem is often affected by how willing we are to stand in our truth. Over time and with conviction to empowerment, you will see yourself detaching more and more to what others say that is in discordance with your value system. No more will others' words have the profound effect they have had on you in the past. Their words will roll off easier without much, if any, emotional upheaval. However, when we are in a fragile place and are constantly hammered with negativity and defeat, it can be very difficult to rise above it alone. It is all about *recognizing* the impact others have on us and *choosing* whether to further consort with them or not.

Most likely there will be naysayers in your community that you cannot or do not want to remove from your life. Quite understandable. I have a few myself. With this type of deal, the best action is to become aware enough to step away from them in times when we are emotionally weak or to avoid certain topics altogether when they are around. We must be conscious enough to limit interaction with those people so as not to allow their negativity to stick to us. I have a person in my life who is quite angry and bitter. I use to take her words as gospel, but as I began to heal, I became repelled by her opinions and beliefs. One day it dawned on me how frightened and armored she is. Since I am in charge of what I allow into my heart, I simply quit attaching to her words and opinions while still loving her. Instead of holding onto her opinions and allowing them to keep me stagnant and afraid, I chose to see her pain and understand that her words would always match her negative vision of the world. Everything that came out of her mouth was a reflection of her sadness and fear. What she said was a reflection of *her* life, not mine.

The time is now to step up and do what's right for you! It's all about moving forward in light regardless what the naysayers in our lives are saying. We may even eventually end up being the pioneer within our own community - the very first person to discover new perspectives and healing tools. When this happens, it can feel quite awkward and uncomfortable at first. However, it's important to understand that you may be the one chosen to bring enlightenment to your circle. Sometimes this new awareness is welcomed and sometimes it will be viewed with contempt or disregard. Whatever the case may be, the key is securing a firm sense of self no matter what the reactions of others will be. Whoever is willing to jump on board with you will, and whoever is not, won't. While in the College of Kristen, I began talking a lot about my new insights and awareness. I was so excited to share all I was learning with the world! Over time, I began to notice that some people wanted to be in it with me and some wanted nothing to do with it. This dynamic was very new to me and initially it took me aback and hurt my feelings. I couldn't yet understand why everyone wouldn't want to be set free! What gave me peace and understanding of this phenomena was later reading an excerpt out of *A New Earth* by one of my favorite mentors, Eckhart Tolle. It went something like this: *When our lights begin to shine, others will either be attracted to us or repelled by us.* Either way it falls, it's not our job to be attached to what others choose for themselves. Our job first and foremost is to love ourselves. If others fall away, an empowered person understands there is a Divine Plan behind it all and she gracefully allows for God's will to be done.

The Truth About Truth Tellers

"You can only rise as high as the tribe you are in."
-Caroline Myss

Oftentimes, individuals who are just beginning the journey to self-empowerment can shy away from people who are truth tellers. At first, truth tellers may feel offensive or threatening when in actuality, the only thing they are *really* threatening is our ego. The ego wants no part of the truth and what will bring us freedom. The ego derives its very life force from our self-lies and unworthiness. When we are weak inside, we tend to believe almost anything that ignites our fears because the ego is trying to strengthen itself. The ego does not want our healing because that would mean its death. With Light/Truth there can be no dark, no ego. Once we attach onto a fearful thought, the ego tries to come up with even more fearful thoughts to support the initial one. Typically fear begets more fear and the vicious cycle begins. We are afraid - we attract more to be afraid of- we are more afraid- we attract even MORE to be afraid of and consequently, we stay completely rooted right where we are! Nothing gained. The truth tellers in our lives serve to challenge all our justifications and excuses which sends our egos spinning into high gear. The truth teller's words may initially ignite defense, denial and/or anger because we have been identified with the ego for so long and consequently, have become "comfortable" in our suffering. The road to empowerment is paved with radical truth - truth that has the capacity to lead us to greater places than we have ever been before. Our truth tellers should be our most valued friends because they are the ones who love us enough to say the hard things.

As with all points of healing, awareness is key. When you observe a moment when your emotional cord has been struck, stop! and ask yourself a couple of questions.

- Was that statement meant to harm me or is this person trying to help me?
- Is it possible that that statement resonated so perfectly for me that it scared me?
- Am I trying to defend my position because I am afraid to move forward and/or because I have become so comfortable in my story?

I completely understand that there are people out there who will say mean things and may not have your best interests at heart. However, sometimes what we may be perceiving as "mean" is actually coming from a very loving place by someone who is trying to help us. *The key is learning to discern between the two.* It is important during this transition period to be very conscious about what others' motives might be when it *appears* they are hurting you. If you get stuck and really don't understand another's motive, don't assume. Ask them to clarify! Many times, what we defend against can be the very thing that can crack our healing vault wide open. Be willing to open your heart to what others are telling you. You might just discover your golden ticket to paradise!

Others Projecting Their Fears

"Don't take anything personally. Nothing others do is because of you. What others say and do is a projection of their own reality, their own dream. When you are immune to the opinions and actions of others, you won't be the victim of needless suffering."
\- Don Miguel Ruiz

It is a common thing for others to project their fear(s) outside of themselves and onto others. For this, it is important that we are mindful of what space others are operating in when discussing our struggles with them. Sometimes people are not completely connected to what we are saying and will respond from ideas/beliefs that are floating around their own heads that really have nothing to do with us. Through their own stories and fears, they are currently viewing the world through a cloudy filter. This is not typically a conscious act on their part, and most often they are clueless to what they are doing. It is *our duty* to recognize when others are not fully present in our conversations and seem to be coming from a perspective that is more pertinent to themselves, rather than us. One might wonder how we can tell the difference. Your God-given intuition, coupled with your physical senses (what you see and hear) will help you realize when someone is coming from their own story rather than fully engaging in yours.

For example, a client of mine made a bold declaration one day that she revisited an old boyfriend many months after their breakup and they ended up having sex that night. She was mortified and literally buried her face in her lap when she told me. She went on to tell me that her friends keep telling her she is being used and she's an idiot for going "there" again. Their words only demonstrated their non-support of her and perpetuated her already low self-esteem. I gently explained to her that for some reason, she must have felt the need to revisit the old relationship. Most likely something was not healed, a lesson not learned or quite simply the relationship was not over. After we coached a little further, she went on to share that that night they ended up having the most intimate and vulnerable conversation they have ever had. She explained how she finally understood why they didn't work out before and how now she felt that she could release him and move on. Because she was supported, she was able to find the blessing in the situation instead of dwelling on the judgments of her cohorts. Without neutral support, she would have most likely beat herself up mercilessly and what potentially could have been gained most likely would have been lost. It's important to note that a positive person will help guide you back to the blessing in the situation. An empowered person will help guide you to your empowerment. A fearful, defeated and victimized person, will guide you to fear, defeat and victimhood.

Client: *I don't know what is wrong with me! I just can't stand to be around negative people anymore!*

My response: *(Smiling big) There is nothing wrong with you! What's happening is that you are strengthening yourself! You have moved up a level of spiritual growth* *and what you used to resonate with, no longer feels right. This means you are healing and no longer will you settle just to fit in. You are right on track!*

How Others May React to Our Growth

"Great spirits have always encountered violent opposition from mediocre minds." – Albert Einstein

Oftentimes when we are growing and evolving, it can feel threatening to the people closest to us. They may feel like we think we are better than them or that we may transform ourselves to a point where we will no longer need or want them in our lives. Ironically, our growth can be quite uncomfortable for some people. For any of the reasons stated, they may attempt to keep us "small" and stuck with them in order to feel safe. By staying in our existing position, we inadvertently provide a safety of sorts to the other person. This does not mean the other person is evil for not wanting our change, it only means they are afraid of what *our* change will bring for *them*. A *Course in Miracles* teaches, there is love and a cry for love. Because they are afraid, they will unconsciously do what they think is best to control the situation in order to keep the perceived security of status quo. In essence, it is not meant to harm you; it is their cry for love.

Ruth is a married, 45 year old woman who had a deep inner urge to write a book (no, this is not me). This was something that she had wanted to accomplish for 20 years. However, her husband, who loved her greatly, kept downplaying the idea. He would tell her how difficult it is to do, how she didn't have the time and how hard it is to get published. Unsurprisingly, she kept putting the book off. His fears amplified her fears. She postponed penning the book for two decades. Ruth was part of a monthly book club. Each month she was surrounded by empowering, reassuring ladies who encouraged and supported her venture. They had the same passion for literature as she did and knew her brilliance. Ruth began to gain her strength and just couldn't hold the book inside any longer. She started to write. It flowed out of her as easily as water flows downhill.

One day, her husband said to her, "If you become a successful author, you will leave me. You won't want me anymore." A-ha! *That* is why he downplayed her idea for so many years! He was afraid. His own fears of his wife's success kept him from supporting her in her dream. (A cry for love) He later confirmed that he knew she could do it, but he was afraid of what her success might do to their marriage.

Ruth later claimed that she felt she wasted a lot time looking outside herself for validation. She was fully aware of her deep, inner urging to become an author, but was doubtful that she could accomplish it and in looking for support and encouragement from her spouse, she got just the opposite. He confirmed her fears instead. She wasn't courageous enough to take the steps needed when *only* talking to him about it, but once she got the support of her book club, she was off and running! Ruth's book became quite a sensation and to the happiness of her husband, the marriage survived her success!

It is so very important to be true to ourselves on our journeys and equally to have open communication with our beloveds. The transformation we are experiencing is not what they are used to and can stir up a lot of fear and upheaval if we don't tend to it. Even though you are growing and changing, your family still needs you and 90% of the drama that happens in households can be bypassed with open communication before the issue reaches a saturation point.

When Shift Happens

"Be the change you wish to see in the world."
-Mohandas Gandhi

Occasionally during our process, it is possible that we may grow apart from others. However, most often we will become a source of inspiration and actually begin to draw people to us. What will determine others' behavior is based *solely* on what is personally going on in their lives at the time. If they are seeking light and healing, most likely they will jump on board. If they are choosing to remain a victim, they most likely will run the other way. It is not something we can control, but it is something we must be aware of in order to not take their behavior personally. Our growth must remain our priority. The complex matrix of the Universe knows what it is doing. Whatever happens, we must have faith that all is in Divine Order. When we act from a place of Love, in this case self-love, it can never be wrong although, it might feel that way when we notice others' discomfort. The doormat's need for approval can kick in right here if we are not aware enough to recognize what is happening.

When I began to transform my life, I began to see

the world through completely different eyes. Assisted by my faith in Source, my spiritual studies and the support of my community, I started detaching from egoic, fearful thoughts and harsh judgments of others and I began to see the world through a clearer lens. I began to change in ways I never even imagined was possible. Watching the people around me during this time was quite fascinating to say the least. Some people were drawn to me like moths to a flame, waiting in baited anticipation for my next word and others began to back away from me. Talk about confusing! But what intrigued me the most, was which ones decided to stay in my life and which ones decided to leave. It was definitely not who I had expected! As time passed, I began to notice how those who stayed began to transform their own lives. Astonishingly, my personal transformation and growth was facilitating healing all around me and reciprocally, *their* transformation and growth was healing me and others around them! What I was witnessing was the most beautiful ripple effect that could potentially reach farther out than I could ever imagine!

Contrarily, those comfortable in their victimhood might slowly fade out of your life. They may stay away for good or they may choose to come back at some point. Whatever they decide to do, has nothing to do with you. I will repeat… It has nothing to do with you and *only* to do with them and where they are on their own spiritual journey. I learned to give others complete personal freedom to be exactly who they are. I allowed them to be at any "place" they currently were on their journey and if that meant leaving our friendship or relationship, it was okay. I would not sit and dwell on the loss, I would send them love and let them go. Sometimes people are in our lives for the long haul and sometimes they are only here for a short period - for us to learn from them, them to learn from us or a combination of the two. We must trust that however long we are graced with their presence is perfect. We were brought together to assist one another's growth on our respective journeys, and when we can allow others to follow their own path without judgment, we are that much closer to enlightenment.

* * *

Surrounding ourselves with positive, loving people can only serve our highest good and help deliver us to the place we are seeking – inner strength, joy and peace. The sure path to reclaiming our lives and learning to love ourselves is brilliantly supported when we have a wonderful set of people around us, who honor all we are, love us unconditionally and care about our growth and well-being. We must be willing to build a strong community and then be fully open to receiving all that that could mean - the validation and the hard truths. Diminishing time spent with people who are unsupportive or negative is okay. It does not mean we hate them or wish them ill will. We are merely taking the steps necessary for loving self-care and creating a life brimming with our manifested desires and dreams.

Thoughts to Ponder: *Who is my current community? Do I feel empowered and inspired after spending time with them? Does my community allow me to grow and evolve? Do I feel supported, valued and loved?*

Set the Intention: *I am deserving of a supportive and loving community. I attract only people of loving character and good integrity into my life. I am open to receiving the love of a supportive community. And so it is.*

Chapter Six

Setting Solid Intentions and Affirmations

"Life does not obey our expectations. Life obeys our intentions, in ways we may not expect". – Lloyd Strom

We hear so much about positivity in today's world although, contrarily, there seems to be a plague of negativity. We hear how staying positive can alter our reality and change our lives yet, we choose every day to join the bandwagon of other people's dramas and continue to speak defeating statements to ourselves and others. Look around you. Have you noticed how the positive, motivated, goal-oriented people seem to find what they are seeking? And the negative, pity-partying ones seem to stay stuck in the same old, tired story of yesteryear? This is simply because we are energetic beings and what we project out into the universe through our thoughts and words, we attract back to us in manifested desires. The ones who are clear and focused are energetically in alignment with their desires and stay connected with the energetic *receiving* of their goal as time passes. They let the Universe decide *how and when* the big ta-da! will happen, while their souls guide their inspiration and creativity. Quite simply, the portion of the population still floundering, uncertain and stagnant, are the ones not using the resources right at their fingertips!

Setting daily intentions and repeating affirmations will… change… your… life! The Universe is willing and able to bring us all that we seek. It is rich with infinite possibilities. It is all about getting clear on what you want to experience, and then choosing a statement to support that goal as if you already have it. Our only job is to align ourselves with our Higher Self and *believe in the deepest core of our being* that we are worthy and deserving of such abundance. To set an intention is to use our free-will to invite the Universe to co-create with us. Without the invitation to assist us, the Creative Forces behind the scenes cannot impose. This is a universal law. When we open ourselves up to receiving and we release the possible ways it will come, fascinatingly, we will begin to notice this divine process in action. Opportunities will begin to arise and a path is laid before us. I have taught this concept to many clients and once they truly understood the energy shift required to attaining their desires, inevitably, what they desired, showed up!

I have a client I'll call Judy. At the time, I had known Judy's for close to 8 years. Throughout that time, Judy had not had a significant other in her life for over 15 years. When we spoke about a potential relationship, she would poo-poo it and say that it really didn't matter to her. As time progressed, I began to intuitively feel that despite her words, this was not true. No matter what words were coming out of her mouth, my intuition told me, she really *did* want a life partner. One day we were on the subject of intuition. I was telling her stories about how my intuition had never failed me and that one of my gifts is to be able to see right through a person and into the truths that they are withholding from themselves. She bravely asked me what I saw/ felt with her. I first asked her if she *really* wanted to know and she agreed. I went on to share how I didn't believe that she didn't want a life partner and how I believed she was blocking the manifestation of such a person because she was afraid. Without any emotion, she inquired further. I went on to say that her fear was stemming from a belief that there are no good men out there and additionally, she was afraid of losing her independence. Unless or until she released these fears, she would continue to be alone. She neither confirmed nor denied my claims.

Six weeks later, we met again. She could hardly contain the smile from her face. "Ok, Judy, what's up with that smile? You met a man didn't you?!" Coyly, she replied, "Yes I did!" I am happy to report it's been almost 3 years and Judy is experiencing the best relationship she has ever had in her life. When Judy recognized her own block and released her fears, the Universe stepped up and handed her the very thing she had desired for so long. The key to manifesting our desires is to simply get out of our own way. What this means is, if we continually undermine our desires, with thoughts of lack and unworthiness, we will never experience them into fruition.

As mentioned earlier, we cannot expect our

manifested desire to come in the precise way we envision. Universal Intelligence has a clear vision of the whole picture and knows precisely how to line it all up. Depending how big the goal, we may be granted only one step at a time - we have to follow the yellow brick road, so to speak. Sometimes the opportunities that present will require us to step out of our comfort zone as Judy was required to do to manifest her dream partner. We must be willing to courageously stretch ourselves and let go of control. If we put all of these wonderful intentions out into the Universe, and not really believe they are possible, we will gain nothing. If we are not in vibrational alignment with our desire, we may be waiting for a very long time.

Affirmations: You are *not* lying to yourself

"If you hear a voice within you saying, 'You are not a painter,' then by all means paint! and that voice will be silenced." –Vincent Van Gogh

I love this quote by Vincent Van Gogh. It clearly tells us how we have the capacity to be anything we want and it is only our minds that tell us it is not so. It's not "who am I to be a painter?" It's "who am I *not* to be a painter?!" The words we speak over our lives have the capacity to lead us to empowerment or keep us stuck. We get to choose our thoughts at any moment, at any time. *Affirmations are modifications of one's belief in self through a chosen set of empowering words.* At first when one begins to speak in positive, powerful affirmations and statements about self, she might feel like it is all a lie. It is important to understand right now, that our lower self (ego) wants to step in and sabotage the growth we are trying to achieve. The "lie" we think we are saying is only our ego trying to keep us small. There is no lie about how magnificent we are or what we are capable of accomplishing! With that being said, if we continue to affirm our worth, our new normal will become thoughts of acceptance and empowerment rather than defeat and lack. We will actually train our brains to think in an entirely different way!

In January of 2011, I made a conscious decision to begin speaking and thinking in affirmations. In the beginning, I thought to myself: *Who am I kidding? This is a joke. I don't believe a word I am saying! These things aren't true!* I wasn't even close to believing the words I was saying; however, I stuck to it. I decided that in order for this to work, I really needed to give myself permission to believe in my worth. I then diligently began to police my thoughts. Each and every time I thought something negative about myself or my life, I immediately turned it around into a powerful affirmation. Seem like a lot of work? It was. However, if you are truly dedicated to your healing, you will gladly do what needs to be done. By week two, I was in absolute awe of the shift in my emotions. I was already noticing that by merely catching my negative thoughts and changing them into positive affirmations, the cloak of depression and unworthiness began to lift from me. I was more peaceful, joyful and a renewed zest for life began to ignite. I began to know with certainty that all this time, I had been my own worst enemy.

By month two, I noticed how my default thought mode was no longer negativity and my *new normal* was self-acceptance and love. I had become gentle with myself and my general mood was reflecting it. I was absolutely fascinated and totally hooked! I couldn't believe how speaking in affirmations could be so powerful. Below I share a sample list of my personal disempowering thoughts and the affirmations I used to replace them.

- I am unlovable. No one will ever want me.

  I am love and I am worthy of love.

- I'm a bitch. No one likes me.

  I am kind and gentle. I am well respected and loved.

- Everyone else gets the good stuff in life. I'm not destined to have the good stuff.

  I am God's child equal to and deserving of abundance as all my brothers and sisters are.

- I am alone. I have no security.

  I have many people supporting me. I am safe.

- I am responsible for other people's feelings.

  I am only responsible for my words. Others are responsible for their feelings.

- I am unworthy of a loving and supportive relationship.

  I deserve to be treated with a high level of love and support in all relationships.

When we speak to ourselves with loving, affirmative words, we empower ourselves in ways we never thought possible or can even imagine. The positive affirmations we speak, transform the negative energy we are experiencing into something powerful and productive. Each and every step we take toward personal empowerment begins within. Affirmations can be used for anything, anytime or anyplace. If you are in doubt, affirm that doubt out! **There is simply no one else who can do this for us.** When we are swimming in the muck of our own self-loathing, it is not our neighbor's words that are going to save us- it is our own.

For example, when I am nervous about attending a new event, my affirmation is:

> *My inner Light shines in all situations.*
> *I am seen for the Light I am.*
> *I am equal to all people. I am safe. And so it is.*

This affirmation immediately draws me back to center and allows me to connect with my Higher Self and genuine nature. I repeat my affirmation as often as needed until I feel my emotions stabilizing. I don't allow for any other thought during this time for to do so would only negate what I am trying to achieve. Consequently, any meeting or outing following this affirmation set is always successful! Most of the drama that occurs in relation to a social event happens first within the mind. So why not quiet the drama happening within the mind *prior* to attending the social event?! When we give ourselves permission to be ourselves, we are more centered, more genuine and our hearts open. This mechanism holds true for *any* situation we may encounter. There is not one situation that we won't benefit from rooting ourselves in love first. If someone tells you affirmations don't work, I can assure you, they are not doing it correctly. By reframing and disciplining the mind, we give ourselves permission to think powerfully and fully own our greatness.

Being gentle, supportive and loving to self, is essential in our evolution. Love is what we need to expand our souls and experience. We must be willing and courageous enough to step out of our boxes and gain forward momentum. If we stand in one place for too long, we grow roots. If we keep doing what we've always done, we will continue to get what we've always gotten. It's so important to try something different to experience the world anew! If you find fear is holding you back, it is time to summon up a little bit of courage and take the first step! Courage has the capacity to amplify our growth and development and will only align us to receiving success in our lives.

Tap Into Your Courage

"Every day we are confronted with hundreds of choices that either make us feel confident, strong, and worthy, or rob us of the things we desire the most. Paralyzing fears, repressed self-confidence, and untapped courage are the obstacles that prevent us from making powerful choices—choices that are in concert with our best interests and deepest desires."
–Debbie Ford

Courage is the driving force behind the process of doormat recovery. It is the one thing we must harness and implement *first* in order to achieve the complete fulfillment of self-love and personal empowerment. It takes great courage to step beyond our conditioned ways of yesteryear and to move into a new way of thinking and acting. It took courage for me to write this book and it took courage for you to read it! Courage may or may not come in one swift, powerful blast. It could present itself in little ways each day where you summon up the strength to take one bold step into the unknown and try something new and different. Since doormat recovery (self-love) varies in degrees from person to person, doing something courageous can differ greatly from person to person. A courageous act will look very different from one person to the next. What may feel like a 2 (easy) on someone's courage scale, may be a 10 (difficult) for you. I can guarantee in other areas your 2 may feel like a 10 to someone else. We are each on our very own specified journey. That is why it's so important not to compare yourself to others or allow others to demean you. You are your own authority.

A wonderful definition for courage is: *feeling the fear and then doing it anyway.* All great rewards take some kind of risk. In order to achieve what we want out of this life, we have to get comfortable with getting uncomfortable. This is not saying we ever put ourselves in harms way. That would not be very self-loving, now would it? Courage is about becoming aware of our fearful places and then pushing past our comfort zones. Exhibiting a little bit of courage every day and then basking in the triumph or outcome, has the capacity to boost our self-esteem immensely! It adds to our list of achievements and those triumphs can quickly become an inspiration for us when we feel like we aren't getting anywhere. We can simply recall a time where we took the leap/risk and gained a great reward afterward. As Debbie Ford once said, *"Unless we are focused on building up our courage, which gives us our self-confidence and all that we need to make quantum change in our lives, the voice of fear will always take the lead inside our minds."* The empowered person knows and understands well her self-limiting past behaviors and knows and understands precisely the steps she needs to take.

Personal Example: *I just couldn't get up in front of everyone and talk tonight, [at my public speaking group] but I am very proud of myself for taking the first step by coming to this meeting! Next time, I will do my best to stand up and share my opinion. My fear will not win nor will I push myself so hard that I never go back.*

You must be willing to be your own cheerleader. Encourage and congratulate yourself for any little (or big) courageous step you make. Your tender support of self is the *very thing* that will catapult you out of your doormathood and into an empowered self. Others' support can and will boost our courage in the short-term and that is a beautiful thing. However, for any lasting effect, we must be willing to do this for ourselves.

How This Works

"The more man meditates upon good thoughts,
the better will be his world and the world at large."
-Confucius

In July 2010, I made this intention:

I am open to new career opportunities coming my
way. I trust that you will bring me only what I am ready
for and I will embrace these opportunities fully. And so it is.

Less than two weeks later I received a random call from an acquaintance of mine. She is Facebook friends with a hostess of a local morning television show here in Phoenix. Apparently, the hostess had posted on her wall that she was looking for a life coach to do a segment on "How to Change Your Life Without Traveling the World." This was during the release of the film, "Eat, Pray, Love" where the main character took a year out of her life to travel to three different countries on a spiritual quest.

I recognized immediately that this was the growth opportunity I had asked for; however, I was scared to death! Historically, public speaking was not my thing! I avoided it in all levels of my education and into adulthood. I would even struggle with something as small as giving a toast! Sooooo… I said yes… and then I freaked out! *Why on earth did I say yes?! This is awful! What was I thinking?! I can't do this!!* I immediately wanted to renege. I was beyond nervous, had *zero* experience public speaking and quite literally I had no idea how I was going to pull this off. My unworthiness, conditioned mind and limiting beliefs were screaming at me and I believed them!

The day of the show, I found myself moving very slowly while my ego kept giving me wonderful ideas of how I could get out of it. *Call them and tell them your child is sick! No, your mom is sick! Your car broke down! You forgot! You are vomiting and have diarrhea! YOU CAN'T DO THIS!* I put off showering and getting ready until the last possible minute. My hands were shaking so terribly, I could hardly put my makeup on straight. *How was I going to do this?!* I successfully got myself ready and began the forty-five minute drive to the station. The entire way there, my ego (lower self) was belittling and demeaning me. *Who do you think you are?! You are not a speaker! What on earth do you think you are doing?! Go home! You don't belong there!* I knew if I didn't get control of my thoughts, I was going to make an enormous fool of myself. I began my affirmations. I repeated them over and over and over again until the moment I walked onto the set.

I am a public speaker. I am well-spoken. I am calm and collected. I exude clarity. I have all the right words to be understood. This is no big deal. I am speaking to friends. I am perfectly safe.

I am happy to report, not only did I not hyperventilate, I delivered a pretty good segment! There was a live studio audience that day that was rapt with attention, laughing at my jokes and connecting to my words. Wow! I did it! To think how my fear/ego was trying to sabotage me, still blows my mind. Had I allowed myself to collapse into the fear, I would have never had such an empowering experience. I also knew that God would not put me in a situation that I could not handle. I had all the tools I needed; I just had to use them. By affirming my worth and being my own cheerleader, I was able to turn my whole experience around. Not only did I get through the segment without disaster, but with all things considered I did a darn good job!

By saying yes to life, a passion ignited in me that I never knew existed. Although I didn't want to admit it to myself, I really enjoyed talking to and teaching a group of strangers. I wanted to become a public speaker! Wait, what?! After returning home, I watched the recorded segment on my television. When it started, I began to feel the panic descend on me all over again, but as the segment rolled, I soon forgot I was watching myself, and I found myself listening intently to what the guest speaker was saying. I realized then: *Wow... I captivated my own attention... I can do this!*

With this new found opportunity in my wake, I took another courageous step and joined a public speaking club. I was still experiencing an overwhelming fear, but I kept pressing on. The entire commute to my meetings, I had to repeat the same affirmation over and over again. I would tremble with the mere thought of standing up to declare my name. However, I knew I could do this, because I already had! Ironically, my affirmations worked so well prior to a speech, no one seemed to notice my fear. What I was feeling on the inside was not prevalent on the outside, at least not to the same magnitude. A few months later after my second speech, a very nervous cohort said to me, "I wish I could do that. How do you do that?!" I couldn't believe that she was asking *me* for help. After all, it was only my second speech! Combined with my TV segments, I had approximately 30 whopping minutes of experience under my belt. My answer was simple: "The only thing I do is talk to myself before every speech. I say positive affirmations until the moment I walk up there." I believe she was hoping for some profound words of wisdom that would rock her world and when I shared "my secret", she just stared at me perplexed and walked away. Through facing one of my greatest fears with affirmations, I learned unequivocally, that we have the capacity to achieve anything we set our minds to. Nothing is unattainable!

Where Do We Start?

"There are only two mistakes one can make along the road to truth; not going all the way and not starting."
-Buddha

One might ask: *What if I don't know what it is I'd like to experience? What if I have no idea what's out in the world for me?* The game plan is to start right smack in the middle with setting an intention. *An intention can be described as modifying our thoughts into alignment with an intended action or behavioral change.* For example:

I am willing and open to new experiences coming my way. I trust in the divine perfection of the Universe in that I will only be presented with experiences and opportunities that will help align me with locating my spiritual gifts and talents. And so it is.

Setting intentions is the direct communication channel to the Universe where we share what we'd like to create and experience in our lives. They can be about anything as long as it's coming from our deepest heart's desire. With this, we open our eyes and minds to a broader view and/or a more unique experience of our lives. We can even start by setting an intention to set more intentions. Any intention is a step forward and forward movement is what we want! The key to personal growth and empowerment is to never stand still. It's about keeping momentum and growth aplenty in our life. It means keeping a lookout for new opportunities and then being willing to say YES when they come.

In my story about the television segment, I had no idea how I could branch out as an empowerment coach/mentor besides one-on-one coaching. I only knew that I wanted to serve others by facilitating faith and empowerment where I could. Additionally, I wanted to work in ways that are exhilarating and exciting. I was unattached to what this was going to look like and I allowed the Universe to take care of it for me. Believe me, if the segment had not presented in the way it did, I know it would not have occurred to me to set one up. However, the Universe heard my call to be of service and divinely put me where It knew I could prevail. I had to trust that the Universe could see what I could not. I had to have faith that any experience brought to me would be exactly what would best serve my evolution. What came from that experience was a zest to teach, a new beginning to my career, and an exciting new prospect for my future. The interesting part is, I was not only led to a great experience, but I was asked back four more times and was referred to another local station for a segment they were doing.

Letting Go

"By letting it go it all gets done. The world is won by those who let it go. But when you try and try, the world is beyond the winning." -Lao Tzu

"Let go" has become somewhat of a catch phrase in our society as of late. Because of this, I feel it may be overused and misunderstood. Let me take a moment to clarify. What does letting go really mean? *Letting go is the releasing of attachment to a certain outcome.* It has also been called "surrender" in some spiritual circles. It is referring to the faith needed by each individual to trust in the Universe to bring to us exactly what is perfect and right for us at this time. After setting an intention, it is of utmost importance that our energy is in vibrational alignment with the absolute manifestation of that desire - feeling "as if" we already have it. Abraham-Hicks, experts in The Law of Attraction, refer to this connection as "the vortex". If we set an intention and then we think to ourselves, *I'll never get what I desire. Things just don't work out for me.* Then guess what? That is exactly what will happen. We must first set the intention, **feel** as though we have received the outcome and then allow the Universe to do its job. Everything comes to us not one minute before it is supposed to. Quantum physics boasts that by giving gratitude in advance for what it is we'd like, the experience will find us. It is not enough, however, to just train your mind to *think* in gratitude and positivity. One must **feel** it. Feeling the energy of having it *before* it's here, is where the energy shift happens. It is resting in the knowledge that there is a process for the development and manifestation of our desires and they may not come in our timing. I have made countless intentions in my life and the ones that were made from a deep place of peace, gratitude and acknowledgement, manifested. The ones that I secretly doubted or possibly didn't really want, did not.

A few years back, I set an intention to experience more male friendships. I have a large community of women but aside from my brothers, I had no male friendships. Being I grew up in a mostly male community, I enjoy and desire male friendships. Men offer different energy and experiences and male-female friendships present many diverse learning opportunities and viewpoints. I had no idea how this would happen because I didn't often go to gatherings where there were a lot of men. I simply stated the affirmation and let it go. Within two months of setting the intention, male friendships started appearing. I began reconnecting with male friends of my past and "magically" a couple of new ones showed up. I now had the male friendships I had desired. I had only set this intention one time and I let go. I had *no doubt* it would manifest and it did.

Intentions and Affirmations as Tools

"Every thought we think is creating our future."
–Louise L. Hay

Whenever we find ourselves in a place in life where we don't seem to have the answers as to what will heal a situation or bring us closer to our goals, setting an intention is the perfect tool! In the beginning they can be vague as long as we start somewhere. When we are truly unsure, we can even set an intention or affirmation to gain clarity such as:

Intention: *I am open to clarity in my life. I am open to receiving the guidance/signs I need to help me discover my passions. And so it is.*

Affirmation: *My mind is open and clear. I see everything in Divine perspective.*

The key is to start *somewhere* and then be willing and OPEN to follow your signs as they come. You will know when you receive a sign because it will show up in such a way that you will think, *"Wow... that cannot be a coincidence"* and/or you will feel a strong pull to follow through with it. God communicates with us in a plethora of ways. We will recognize the message by the way it feels. Learning to retrain our thinking and refraining from negative self-talk is one vital key to transforming our personal power. What we repeat, we learn. What we repeatedly say to ourselves, we will eventually believe. By repeating our affirmations and intentions, we are teaching ourselves daily how amazing and powerful we are. Dr. John Demartini, a human behavioral specialist, international educator, published author and an authority on maximizing human awareness, has said that he has so many affirmations that if he recorded them all back to back, there would be enough to fill a 24 hour period! One affirmation in particular he has repeated **daily** for 42 years: *I am a genius and I apply my wisdom.* This affirmation was born at the young age of 17 when through the guidance of a mentor, he was asked to declare what he would like to dedicate his life to. His answer was, *"I am going to become a teacher, healer, and philosopher. I will find a way to travel the world and set foot upon every country across the face of the earth, share* *my research with others, and help everyone live inspired and magnificent lives."* To expand further, Dr. Demartini was told in first grade that he would never read, write or communicate effectively. He didn't actually learn to read until he was 18 years old. However, through affirmation and intention, he not only learned to read and write, he went on to medical school and later became one of the most successful authors and public speakers of all time! He manifested his dream life because he affirmed it so.

When we speak powerful affirmations all day, every day, eventually, there will be no choice than to start believing it. When we clean up our inner dialogue and perceptions, we cease to see ourselves through the filthy filter of yesterday but through a fresh and clear new filter that embodies our genius within. With this, better decisions are made regarding our lives and our faith in self rises to levels that we have never known before. Amazing things begin to happen when we choose to honor (and fully believe in) not only our worth, but the abundance of the Universe. It is up to us, and only us, to do the work to take care of the very essence of our being, our beautiful soul.

"We were birthed with one soul to take care of and we must take care of it." -Debbie Ford

Thoughts to Ponder: *Do I take responsibility for the words I speak over my life? Do I worry too much "how" things are going to manifest rather than having faith in the Divine? Do I understand the law of free-will and how I must invite in assistance?*

Set the Intention: *Begin by getting focused and clear about a desire that you would like to attract into your life. Be mindful and present when you set your intention and then let go… End each intention with "And so it is." In this, we are sealing our words to God.*

Chapter Seven

Meditation & Contemplation- Making Space for Our Messages

"To end the misery that has afflicted the human condition for thousands of years, you have to start with yourself and take responsibility for your inner state at any given moment. That means now." –Eckhart Tolle

"Meditation brings wisdom; lack of meditation leaves ignorance. Know well what leads you forward and what holds you back, and choose the path that leads to wisdom." -Buddha

It has been said that one's mind is like a bowl of rice. If the bowl is full, it cannot accept anymore. If our minds are too cluttered with out-of-control fear thoughts and un-serving beliefs, we have no room left for the emergence of Truth or Divine Creation. In the day to day grind of life, inner peace and guiding messages can be drowned out in the cacophony of noise we have in our minds. When reclaiming one's personal power, emotional health and wholeness, it is of primary importance to be able to hear our true inner expressions and guidance of Source. We must be willing to allow for space for our messages- our deepest knowing- our intuition. By creating gaps in our over-thinking minds, we bring forth the necessary "quiet" so needed to connect with our Higher Selves and to invite forward new information and insights. A clear mind provides the ideal setting to become better acquainted with one's true, genuine nature and functions in alignment with peace and Divine Inspiration. It opens the mind and heart to new perspectives and consequently facilitates a more empowered path forward. As we adopt a meditation practice into our lives, our "new normal" becomes a quiet mind.

Meditation (and contemplation) begets patience, balance, inner peace and harmony. It is the practice of clearing the mind through deep, mindful breathing, mantras and/or visualization methods. It silences the left brain (thinking and analyzing) and releases the energy of our right brain (intuition and creativity). Meditation is about achieving a higher state of consciousness through stillness and the allowance of the Holy Spirit's presence in our lives. It takes away the incessant babble in our minds, giving us rest from ourselves and allows us to hear the gentle guidance available to us. It brings about inner strength and fortifies our mind power.

Contemplation is the process of getting quiet through deep breathing and relaxation and then pondering a chosen subject. It is a gentle stream of thought without judgment or attachment to any specific outcome. It is granting ideas and insights passage to flow gracefully through our minds. It is the common place where creativity is born and inspiration arises. It is by definition an "unhurried focus".

Meditation and contemplation often go hand in hand. Many times while meditating, we can slip into contemplation mode. As long as we are quiet in mind and allowing for the flow, we are benefiting from our practice. We must not judge ourselves as to how it goes, but to allow our practice to unfold as it will. The key is to release ourselves from worry and control if even for only moments at a time. Settling the mind for even thirty seconds at a time can seem like an arduous task to some. Be gentle with yourself and know that you are *practicing* a new skill and as with all things, it will take some time to get better at it. Remember, no master became a master overnight.

As our practice strengthens, we may use meditation and contemplation as our "go to" place when we are seeking answers. It is important to keep in mind, our messages may or may not come in the precise moment of meditation and contemplation nor will they always be what we are expecting or wanting to hear. The goal of this practice is to provide space for the guidance (whatever it will be) to be heard and when it does come, trust it and then choose a supportive action. A couple years ago, I found myself struggling terribly with a situation. The situation made me very nervous and I was grappling to do the right thing. One day I decided to meditate on it. During the meditation I was greeted with a Light Being. It was something I had never experienced before. This being was in the "form" of a peace-filled, shapeless, white, androgynous, cloud-like figure. I began to ask the Light Being for help. The message he/she kept repeating was: *You are doing everything right.* I remember there being a little more dialogue; however, the repeating message was: *You are doing everything right.* After my meditation I sat quietly and reflected on that message. *Wow... That was weird... Was that real? Should I believe this message? Why wasn't there more? Why wouldn't he/she explain it further to me?* Since the answers to those questions were not provided, I decided to embrace the message I *did* receive. What came from that was me giving myself permission to relax about the situation by letting go of outcome because I unequivocally knew *I had done everything I could.* What I received was confirmation that the situation was not about *my* behavior and choices, but about the other person's behavior and choices. Spirit knew that what I needed to hear in order to let the situation go, was that there was nothing I had the power to do that could change it.

Additionally, sometimes the messages we receive are not what we want to hear and our ego can trick us into thinking the guidance is not true. This can cause us to remain stuck in anxiety and fear over the situation. In the aforementioned story, I was very hung up on a certain guy. I meditated like crazy hoping that through silencing my mind chatter, I would get the answer I wanted - that he was "the one" for me. What I repeatedly got was the exact opposite; a deep inner knowing that moving on was the best option. I fought this message like mad because I *perceived* I had control which only perpetuated my uncertainty and fear. Inevitably, the relationship ended, but not before causing tremendous amounts of emotional upheaval in my life. Spirit could see the situation clearly, but I could not. By becoming more open to our guidance, we will begin to understand our connection to Source in a much deeper way. Our outcomes will begin to match the messages received and we will naturally become more trusting of the Universe. Whatever our inner voice may be saying, we will learn to trust it as we become more familiar with the "feeling(s)" associated with the delivery of the message. As our practice deepens and we begin to trust and act from our inner knowing, what used to cause much effort and stress in our lives will be replaced with peace and natural order.

What Does Meditation Feel Like?

"I'm simply saying that there is a way to be sane. I'm saying that you can get rid of all this insanity created by the past in you. Just by being a simple witness of your

thought processes. It is simply sitting silently, witnessing the thoughts, passing before you. Just witnessing, not interfering not even judging, because the moment you judge you have lost the pure witness. The moment you say "this is good, this is bad," you have already jumped onto the thought process. It takes a little time to create a gap between the witness and the mind. Once the gap is there, you are in for a great surprise, that you are not the mind, that you are the witness, A watcher. And this process of watching is the very alchemy of real religion. Because as you become more and more deeply rooted in witnessing, thoughts start disappearing. You are, but the mind is utterly empty. That's the moment of enlightenment. That is the moment that you become for the first time an unconditioned, sane, really free human being." -Osho

Meditation has been described by many spiritual masters in beautifully poetic ways. In simplistic terms, I define it as: *Quieting the mind through visualization, repeated mantras, breath and presence.* I have heard many people say, "I can't meditate! It's impossible for me!" Meditation and contemplation may not be easy at first, but in time, it can become a highly loved and valued practice in one's life. No one is exempt from being able to have a beneficial meditation practice. However, it doesn't just happen! One must be willing to understand the benefits, dedicate herself to the goal and learn to discipline her mind.

Oftentimes throughout our day, we may be in meditation mode without even knowing it. Take a moment to draw up a memory of a time when you were daydreaming. Do you remember how your thoughts ambled by without you attaching to or judging any one? This is what Osho so beautifully describes as being "the witness" in the above quote. It is the times we are relaxed enough to clear our minds completely and let our messages/creativity come through organically. It is the times where we merely *observe* the thoughts passing by without giving them identity or life. That is what meditation and contemplation feels like. Think again back to your daydream experience. Do you remember the feeling of complete freedom as your mind wandered from subject to subject and idea to idea? How many wonderful ideas came through while you were daydreaming? Probably quite a few because that is the time our minds are quiet and open. Inspiration is born in a quiet mind. It is the place where we connect to the source of Infinite Wisdom and

Universal Knowledge. When we quiet our mind chatter, we can hear our soul speaking. Our soul holds all our answers, inspirations, faith and creativity toward our life's path. When we take the time to create the space, it allows for unseen energies to emerge. Meditation and contemplation can feel so wonderful, that sometimes one won't even want to return to the physical plane because of the peace and clarity that arises. However, do not fret. Through continued practice, we can learn to carry that same feeling into our day to day existence. Life doesn't have to be hectic. There **is** a way!

"Why do we meditate? We meditate precisely because this world of ours has disappointed us and because failure looms large in our day-to-day life. We want fulfillment. We want joy, peace, bliss and perfection within and without. Meditation is the answer, the only answer." -Sri Chinmoy

When I was in the midst of my tsunami, I felt extreme anxiety and fear like I had never experienced in my life. My body trembled, my mind was jumbled and confused and I could hardly finish (or begin) the simplest tasks. I looked right through my children and I felt completely out of balance. I even remember at certain times the muscles in my upper lip contracting and pulling up involuntarily at the left corner as if in an Elvis sneer. Never before had I experienced such anxiety and emotional weight. This feeling was very foreign, uncomfortable and almost unbearable! I didn't know what to do with myself, much less with my children. I knew I had to get myself balanced soon or I was going to make some terribly bad decisions. I began to pray and ask God for help.

All at once, I remembered my kundalini yoga classes and how at the end of every session we would sit in mediation while the yogi would play the gong. I would leave the studio in a state of complete peace. I had experienced, for probably the very first time, what emotional freedom and peace really felt like. Although I was new to the practice and I didn't yet understand the massive benefits of meditation, I did finally understand what a state of "being" meant. I recognized in an instant, this was my answer! I made a decision to immediately begin meditating.

Note: It's important to recognize the recall of my gong meditation experience. I had been asking God for help and surely, the answer came. Oftentimes, we receive these types of messages, but quickly shirk them off as *unimportant. We think we need to have cognitive control over our lives at all times and/or we do not recognize the importance of the messages we are receiving. My answer didn't come in the way I had expected, but remember, our guidance usually only imparts **our next best step** and my next best step, at that time, was to get quiet and connected!*

I'm not saying starting to meditate is going to be super easy. Meditation and contemplation can *seem* very difficult at first. I implore you though, to keep to it! Do not criticize yourself or become disempowered if you struggle to maintain focus. It is a *practice* and you **will** get better! Do not give up on yourself. Not only are you creating peace and calm in your life, you are training yourself to control your thoughts and emotions for future situations as well. Simply know that learning this method will bring you future fulfillment in all that you do. Meditation and contemplation are extremely beneficial in creating a whole and sound life. Simply, there are only benefits that come from it.

Relinquish Control by Becoming the Observer

"The mind can go in a thousand directions, but on this beautiful path, I walk in peace. With each step,

the wind blows. With each step, a flower blooms."
-Thich Nhat Hanh

"I do not want to foresee the future. I am concerned with taking care of the present. God has given me no control over the moment following."
–Mohandas Gandhi

We as human beings, feel a continual need to attempt to control the happenings around us. We mistakenly believe we can control *all* aspects of our lives. Although this holds true is some aspects (for example: what we eat or drink or how much we exercise), it is untrue in many other areas. There are situations that arise in our lives that we simply have no control over. The only control we do have during those rough times is how we respond. For example, there was no way I could control the forces of my tsunami. The storm had begun and it was gaining force. The only "control" I conceivably had was how I handled my emotions, my thoughts and my behavior. By learning to become present with "what is", I learned to relinquish control and flow more gracefully with the tides. In the above quote by Mohandas Gandhi, he states, "God has given me no control over the following moment." I interpret this to mean, we do not have control over anything but this very moment and to think otherwise is to cause ourselves unnecessary suffering. When one is completely enmeshed in a moment of presence, there is no room to be disgruntled or upset because in pure presence, there is no suffering. We merely become the observer of our surroundings and experience. When we allow for the unfolding of situations without the illusion that we can somehow control outcome, our heart centers open and we are unobstructed in our decisions and behaviors.

I remember that during the meditation portion of the kundalini class, the yogi asked us to "become the observer". I had no idea what that meant! I remember thinking, *"Observe what? I'm supposed to be meditating; doesn't that mean just clearing my mind?"* I had always understood meditation as being a place of no thought. However, over time I began to notice that when my mind was quiet, thoughts, ideas and insights seemed to flow by like a lazy river. I did not emotionally *attach* to anything. I merely *observed* them as they entered and exited my mind while I remained at peace. It felt similar to idly riding passenger in a car and watching the scenery outside the window pass by. We don't try to control the scenery, nor do we try to attach any emotion to it - we merely observe it. My mind would fall into a peaceful observation place where nothing that passed through elicited an emotional reaction. Recalling those moments in class, I further decided this was unequivocally my answer.

I began to meditate and contemplate as often as I could. I would practice on the floor in my house, a lobby or waiting room, my car, the back patio and even occasionally on the treadmill at the gym (holding on to the rail of course!). When I say I was dedicated to finding my peace, I mean I was DEDICATED. Oftentimes, our human need to control inhibits us from a productive meditation practice. We are so busy white knuckling our situations that we don't want to let go for one measly second in fear we may completely lose control. Meditation gives us that much needed break from our minds even if for only small increments at a time. It's important during our meditation time, that we give ourselves permission to let go of our problems **for now.** By telling ourselves it is *"just for now"*, I believe we satisfy our forceful ego for a little while which frees up the control our mind so desperately wants to have. Afterwards, if we see fit, we can return to the problem at hand. However, I soon discovered that as I deepened my practice, my obsessive need to control began to fall away. Additionally, with consistent practice, we might notice that when we do return to the issue, it feels much lighter and way more manageable!

"Whenever an answer, a solution, or a creative idea is needed, stop thinking for a moment by focusing attention on your inner energy field… When you resume thinking, it will be fresh and creative."
–Eckhart Tolle

Incorporating a daily meditation and contemplation practice into our lives helps us get in touch with presence and leads us to a more peaceful existence while dealing with the physical world around us. It is proven that when we are calm and centered we make better decisions and our physical body is enhanced as well. With the reduction in fear and anxiety, the body is strengthened. Our immune system is enriched and it has been proven that even some chronic illnesses have been alleviated in the bodies of people whose minds are at peace. The mind/body relationship is so intimately connected, that healing one can heal the other. Meditation allows for a "quiet power" to come into our lives and can literally begin to heal our mind, body and Spirit.

How to Meditate

"If we know the divine art of concentration, if we know the divine art of meditation, if we know the divine art of contemplation, easily and consciously we can unite the inner world and the outer world." - Sri Chinmoy

Meditation is not about perfection. There are many people out there who have been meditating for years and still cannot reach a "mastered" state. It could take months or even years to be able to meditate at a level of whole-mindedness and you still may not be able to fully master it in this lifetime. This does not mean, however, that you are not gaining the massive benefits that accompany the practice. Any amount or type of meditation is better than none at all. As Remez Sasson, an author and expert on spiritual growth and consciousness, so succinctly states, *"Even masters had to take the first step, so can you."*

Below is an example of a simple meditation that can get you started on your practice today. Remember, it's not about *how* you mediate only that you do.

To begin:

1. Locate a quiet place where you will not be disturbed or have outside distractions such as phones ringing or doorbells. Decide upon the amount of time you would like. Five to twenty minutes is a great starting place. *Note: First thing in the morning is an ideal time to connect with Spirit and to initiate peace and stillness throughout your day.*

2. Choose a comfortable position to meditate in. You may choose to lie down or sit upright. Loosen any tight or constricting clothing and remove hair ties or accessories that might be pulling or distracting in anyway.

3. Close your eyes and begin breathing slowly and regularly. Begin to inhale as deeply as you can through your nose and exhale as slowly as you can through your mouth. *When we are highly stressed we tend to breathe shallowly or pant like a dog.* Our breathing is very important. It not only can relieve anxiety quickly, it delivers necessary oxygen to our cells for optimal physiological function.

4. Become aware of your breathing as it gets deeper and notice how your heart rate slows down. With each inhale, count "one" and with exhale, count "one" up to number ten and then back down to one again. If you lose your place, start again at "one". You may also choose to repeatedly say your name, an affirmation or chosen mantra while you concentrate on the life force you are breathing into your body. Feel the tension ease out of your body as you quiet your mind.

Example Affirmation: *All is well. All is at peace. I relinquish control of my life while I take this time for me. My problems and issues can sit without my supervision for this moment.*

Example Mantra: *I am loved and I am safe.* When you feel your body has relaxed, you can either continue to control your breath or return naturally to your involuntary breathing pattern.

5. Allow yourself to drift into the world of contemplation/observation. You are the creator of your experience. There is no wrong way. If

your mind keeps returning to stressful thoughts or the need to control, simply recognize the thought as you would a small child pulling on your skirt at an inopportune time and tell it, "Not now". At the end of your practice allow yourself to return to the physical world through slow and easy movements. Try to maintain your quiet mind as you return to your daily activities.

One may also choose a visualization practice. With this, many like to imagine themselves taking a peaceful journey along a stream through the woods or watching the sun set over the ocean. Whatever fills your heart and soul with peace and helps facilitate presence within, is what is perfect for you. How you design your meditation is yours to decide. *This is your time.* There is a time and purpose for everything and this time and purpose is for **you** to love and nurture yourself by creating balance and harmony in your life.

If you wish to deepen your practice, local booksellers carry many books on the subject. There are guided meditation CD's, mp3 downloads and YouTube has a wonderful selection of guided meditation videos. Some people prefer something akin to the above mentioned method with complete silence or new age music softly playing in the background. Others may prefer a guided mediation. Simply knowing there is not a wrong way to meditate takes the pressure off of "doing it right". Many people are so concerned with doing it right that they sabotage their practice before they begin. I implore you to be gentle with yourself during this process. Give yourself the grace you deserve while you are learning a new skill. Eventually with practice you will find it easier to reach your center within and without meditation. You may do it while sitting in an office waiting room or shopping in a crowded store. Through practice you will be able to call upon your peace at will whenever you start to feel out of balance.

"A beginner needs a quiet place to meditate. Someone with a lot of practice can meditate everywhere and under all circumstances." –Remez Sasson

I invite you to record (keep a journal) of any inspirations, ideas or a-ha's you may have gotten during your meditation/contemplation to reflect upon later. It is inspiring and faith building to look back as your life progresses and you bear witness to your evolution. When we learn to trust ourselves, our confidence and self-esteem grow. You may also find yourself receiving intuitions that later come to fruition. Referring back to your entries will help you gain trust in your messages as you watch what you previously recorded becoming true. Be open to anything that comes your way even if it initially does not seem to fall in line with your beliefs or traditional thought patterns. This may be your Higher Self raising your consciousness outside the parameters that you are used to functioning in. Allow your presence and breath to be the portal for a new life of peace, clarity and insight.

Recognize and Celebrate the Change!

"To say, 'well done' to any bit of good work is to take hold of the powers which have made the effort and strengthen them beyond our knowledge."
–Phillips Brooks

Through practicing quiet mind, we will find ourselves responding to situations rather than reacting. We discover a greater patience and a better understanding of "loving what is". We learn that the answers we are seeking become readily available when we quiet the mind. By maintaining a centered core being, upsetting events, anxiety and emotional outbursts are decreased greatly. Quite often since the onset of my tsunami, I observed myself in various scenarios where an emotional, old reaction of the past would cease to emerge. Something was shifting within me and I liked it! I was also quite astounded how I flowed more easily with life ups and downs. It's so important on the road to empowerment to celebrate your changes! Not just with meditation, but each and every time you choose an empowered move over a weak-minded move. Recognition allows us to see the benefits and helps us to continue forward.

Learning to "let go" and inviting God's guidance in, gives a sense of security that honestly, many of us on the planet have never truly felt or understood. I, for one, was astonished how much confidence and faith I began to put into God when I could finally hear my messages and navigate my life more peacefully. I celebrated the fact that I was no longer bound to my past behavioral patterns - that there was indeed a better way! The truth is, I hadn't let go of them, they had let go of me! I learned that finding my inner peace was crucial in maintaining a neutral balance and making great decisions no matter how important or trivial the decision is. My behavioral shift was unmistakably demonstrating this to me. With almost no effort, I had discovered a new, better and gentler way of handling my life.

Over time, we also might begin to know/see/feel that we do not have to react BIG to the stressors in our lives. We can feel the emotion, let it be what it is and use it to serve as a guide as to what is not being met in our lives. We will learn that the observer position is much more beneficial than the stressed out reactor position. This is not to say we become perfect and will never have difficult moments or make mistakes. We are still human and we are still fallible. Perfection is not our goal. However, learning to quiet the fearful mind and debilitating thoughts *is* our goal. Meditation and contemplation are essential tools in leading us to living a soulful, spiritual and empowered life. Dr. Brian Weiss states in *Same Soul, Many Bodies*, *"Live this moment, this precious, unique moment of grace, light, and freedom, by surrendering to it."*

Thoughts to Ponder: *Do I find myself obsessively overthinking situations hoping I can control them somehow? Am I so fogged up with fear, anxiety or* *heavy emotion that I may not even be hearing God communicating with me? Is my typical way of handling stress and difficult situations working for me on all levels?*

Set the Intention: *I am open to clearing my mind of clutter so that I may be open to the peace and clarity of God's guidance in my life. I say yes to harmony and balance as I incorporate a lifestyle of quiet mind. And so it is.*

Chapter Eight

No More Compromising Your Sacred Self

"While we try to connect with another's heart beat we are half a person. When we connect with our own heart beat we are whole." -Marianne Thorne

I understand the yearning and desire for a life partner or mate. I understand the human need for security, companionship, attention, love and touch. It is part of the human experience to want coupling and/or companionship. In Abraham Maslow's list of man's hierarchy of needs, security and safety are *only* preceded by breathing, food, water, sex, homeostasis, sleep and excretion. A great sense of security can accompany a relationship because it is something we innately crave. I believe a human being finds much comfort in feeling like we don't have to brave this life alone and that we belong somewhere to someone. I get it. I am human too. However, looking back over your life, to what extent have you compromised your sacred self in order not to be alone? Perhaps you can recall a relationship where you initially thought everything was going great only to eventually discover that your commitment, love and time were simply not valued. I can bet you stayed much longer than you should have because at the time, having someone might have appeared better than having no one or the fear of leaving outweighed the pain of staying.

Doormats are often willing to go against their own moral code and self-worth just to feel needed, wanted or accepted.

In relationships such as these, doormats tend to fall completely out of alignment with themselves. They make self-defeating compromises and exceptions where they shouldn't. Disrespectful or unloving behavior from others becomes standard acceptance protocol because we believe through the subconscious filter of our unworthy selves, that this might be as good as it gets. Oftentimes when asked by others why we condone another's crappy treatment, we use denial statements like: *"He's really a good person on the inside."* Or *"Because I love him."* Or *"I'm just easy going, it doesn't really bother me."* Or *"He's getting better."* Or *"You just don't know him like I do."* We deceive ourselves into accepting the unacceptable just to stay "connected" to another person. Little do we know that each day and each disrespectful act is eating away at our worth. I have experienced this repeatedly throughout my own life and I have witnessed it a zillion times in other people's. I feel it important to state that the acceptance of the unacceptable is not only true for women. It is equally true for men. Anytime one partner (male or female) puts up with disrespect or dishonor, he/she has given away his/her power.

Let us also be aware that mistreatment and abuse doesn't always show up in physical form. It can show up in a plethora of ways such as: humiliation, criticizing, negating, domination, shame, silent treatments and/ or emotional abandonment or neglect. In order to recover from years of accepting the unacceptable, it is of utmost importance to admit to yourself the truth of your pattern and make the commitment right here, right now, that it is no longer acceptable.

Short-term Gratification vs. Long-term Pain – Why we linger

"From a distance it is something; and nearby it is nothing." -Jean de LaFontaine

Even in nonreciprocal relationships there are going to be moments of short-term gratification. For example, your person may be fun, great in bed, spend money on you, complimentary at times or take you traveling. This is precisely why we may start compromising our sacred self because it *appears* we are getting something. We take the *something* and we internalize it as "love" and we begin making excuses as to why the rest of his unacceptable behavior is okay. We allow ourselves to be distracted by the hoopla even though the hoopla is only superficial (not Real Love) and will only last for moments at a time. We make bargains in our minds and excuse away anything unacceptable because the thought of being alone is horrifying. However, over time the result is a weakening of our spirit, strength, self-esteem and confidence because our true value is not being honored by our partner or ourself. Deep inside we feel empty, forgotten and unimportant. The very thing we are seeking (security) has backfired in a big way.

In most cases, we try to convince ourselves that *our* wonderful love can change our partner or that the situation isn't as bad as it seems. We focus only on the "good" aspects of the person and we attempt to justify the rest. We may also tend to blame ourselves in order to keep the spotlight off of our partner's inadequacies. Either way, security remains ever elusive and the lack of connection becomes quite evident. After the superficial "high" begins to fade away, we are left with reality and we just can't seem to escape the feeling of sadness. We notice in the grand scheme, our needs and wants truly do not matter. We may have a warm body to lie next to at night or have someone to do things with, but the profound sense of unfulfillment is undeniable. Our heart lacks the nurturing it desires and we are missing the deep, honest, spiritual connection that our souls are yearning for. In due course the relationship becomes lopsided, non-cohesive and unbearably painful.

I remember in the months following the end of a 10 year relationship, I quickly began to date a man I will call Dick. Dick was good looking, great in the sack and had money. He always had tickets to some great event and superficially all seemed well. One evening, only a short time into the relationship, we were sitting on his sofa watching TV and he got up and went into the kitchen. He came back with a heaping bowl of ice-cream with hot fudge. I nicely asked him why he didn't offer me any and he said with a sneer on his face, "If you want some, go get it yourself." Within my value system, if you are helping yourself to something, you always ask your guest if she'd like some too. I considered this disrespectful and inconsiderate and I promptly got up and headed for the door. He jumped up, stopped me and asked where I was going. I told him that his behavior was rude and not the way I wanted to be treated. I left. But not before I angrily left a huge burnout in his perfectly manicured gravel driveway. Little did I know at the time that his "ice cream behavior" only served as the straw that broke the camel's back. You see, other things had already happened that I was subconsciously ignoring and excusing away and because I had refused to recognize these issues, my reaction steeped with suppressed emotion. For example:

1. He hardly called and if he did, the conversation lasted approximately 5 minutes.
2. He never made dates in advance. He always called last minute.
3. He never asked questions about me or recognized my uniqueness and value.
4. He never spoke about the future.
5. He had no interest in learning more about my children or my dreams.

On some level, I could already see and feel that he wasn't honoring me as a committed partner (using me), but I still chose to engage with him (short-term gratification). I had held back my feelings and experience of him up until that point (to refrain from pushing the limits) because having him appeared better than being alone. I had already assigned him to potentially be "the one" and I was willing to compromise myself in order to make sure that happened!

To break down the "ice cream situation" a little further, my idea was on course (recognizing his disrespect), my words perfectly stated (succinct and to the point) and although the burnout was definitely not necessary (hey, it is what it is!), I did the right thing by finally not accepting disrespectful treatment. What happened after that was when I became the doormat! The next day I dropped the ball big time by not standing behind my words with action. I waited anxiously for his call, I jumped to answer the phone when the call came in and I gave in immediately following an absurdly short apology and almost no conversation regarding the subject. I had already made all kinds of excuses for his behavior and I believed them. I was sickly sweet on the phone and I just couldn't wait to see him again. I wanted him to accept and love me! Ewwww! What an empowered person would have done is:

- Not waited around for the call and only answered if the timing was right
- Listened openly to his apology
- Took time to process the underlying messages of his behavior
- Took time to clear her head and heart
- Stepped back a bit from the relationship until it was shown through action and words that the lesson was learned

Deep inside I knew I had not gained any respect with my comportment, but only succeeded in showing him my lack of self-respect. But I didn't care. I was only interested in the moments of short-term gratification that I was getting - the occasional phone calls, the last minute dates and the sex. What Dick learned through that episode, was that he could treat me disrespectfully and I would give in without any responsibility taken on his part. What little respect for me he may have had in the beginning, faded quickly and I secured my position as his doormat. In essence, whatever he said or did, I accepted and I hid under the guise of, "Eh, I'm just a forgiving person." *When we are "needy", we are willing to believe any lie we tell ourselves in order not to lose the relationship.* We compromise our sacred self at almost any cost. Although he may have been attracted to me in the beginning, when I gave him total power over me, I can assure you, I quickly became unappealing.

In lopsided situations such as this, we can also become clingy in an effort to force the security, love and attention that we so long for. With this, the energy we emit toward the relationship begins to repel our partner. Eventually, we begin to feel his detachment or pulling away and the downward... spiral... begins. We cling, they push, we cling, they push and each time we feel further rejected, our self-esteem plummets lower.

Low self-esteem only serves to perpetuate the same behavior and an even lower self-esteem will ensure the perpetuation of the same behavior! We may start to think that if we could only be prettier, smarter, more fun, sexier etcetera then he will value us. Our mind (ego) begins to play tricks on us and we think the problem lies in the outside world instead of our inside world. We are clueless to the fact that we can never fill ourselves up by another. We try too hard and compromise ourselves in ridiculous ways in hopes of keeping the relationship and maintaining the illusion of love and security. We begin to shift into a new role based on our *perceived notion* of what our partner wants and we cease to honor any part of our authentic selves. We move farther and farther away from our true nature which eventually leads to a disconnection of mind, body and spirit.

How to Stop the Madness

"Until you know Beloved, that who you are -just as you are- is enough to sustain you, you can't see God or anyone else." - Iyanla Vanzant

We stop the madness by learning to love and honor ourselves first and foremost. We start to realize, above all else, that we are God's child - wholly deserving of the abundance that life has to offer. We are whole and perfect just as we are and love and respect is our birthright. When we deviate from this inner knowing (or never knew it in the first place), we continually seek outside for what has been lying in wait all along - the love inside us that is the very essence of our being. The very nature of our being already knows the truth of Who we are and subconsciously we feel guilty because something inside knows it is we who are not taking care of God's beloved child. Eventually, our shame and guilt can manifest in a perpetual dark cycle of self-loathing, unworthiness and pain. Our dim light becomes darker thus repeating the same patterns in our lives. The only way up and out of the pit, is self-love and self-care! True, genuine, loving care of self is about treating ourselves the same as if we are caring for a small child. Self-respect and love will not allow for someone to treat us poorly. It is a natural phenomenon. It is through hardcore self-evaluation and a commitment to our healing, that we truly tap into the essence of our divine selves and stop our neurotic behavior once and for all. Once we realize and own the fact that we are worthy of a great love and *we only possess the power to change ourselves*, we are half way there! Loving and honoring yourself through appropriate choices and loving self-talk, is the utmost priority in healing from and transcending the vicious cycle of disproportionate relationships. Knowing deep within how worthy you **really** are, is key to stopping the madness once and for all.

Oftentimes, many people will want to blame the man or woman they are dating or married to or simply consider it bad luck.

I always attract the jerks/bitches/psychos/ narcissists/non-committers etc. I'm just unlucky!

In doing this, the ego is trying to keep the focus off of you and put it onto the other person. I'm here to tell you, it is not about the other person nor is it bad luck. It is all about us. We are the ones who allowed the behavior to continue. The Universe will continually provide the perfect classroom(s) to learn in by giving us partners that will reflect back our wounded places. If we keep the focus off our behavior and only on the other person's, we cannot discover the means that will help us transcend this pattern once and for all.

Once we begin to strengthen ourselves, we will no longer cower to avoid pushing the limits of the relationship. An empowered person will understand that we must be willing to speak up and back up our speech with action in order to preserve our sacred self. Additionally, she will have determined an "Unacceptable Treatment Guideline" in which to live by. In this, she will have set standards for herself where she is unwilling to compromise whatsoever. For example:

Unacceptable Treatment Guideline Sample:
1. Substance abuse or addictions
2. Cheating
3. Consistency of other priorities over the relationship
4. Physical or emotional abuse
5. Chronic lying
6. Unwillingness to take ownership of wrong doings

The list doesn't have to be long as long as it's true for you and you are willing to stand behind it. The most important part is getting crystal clear about what types of behavior you will no longer accept. Once we begin to live within the boundaries of our guideline, we may find potential partners coming in and going out more quickly than in the past. We might try to view this as bad or as if it's our fault and there is something wrong with us. It is of utmost importance to know that when someone leaves your life because you have set a boundary, that person is only showing that he is not the one for you. His exit is your gift! When I first began dealing with this, I would question myself: *Maybe I'm wrong. Maybe I'm being too harsh. Maybe if I allowed his behavior, it would be okay.* Yikes! Do not be alarmed if you find yourself attempting to back down. Simply become aware and understand it will take time to strengthen this muscle. In the meantime, congratulate yourself for having the courage to protect your sacred self from an unsavory character! With this, you have just aligned yourself with something bigger and better to come. When we allow the "unacceptables" to leave, we have advanced ourselves steps closer to our sweet empowerment. With each step, we are strengthening our self-worth and making the necessary changes to breaking this pattern for good!

Aloneness = Re-Creation Time

"But if you have nothing at all to create, then perhaps you create yourself." -Carl Jung

Historically, when a romantic relationship ended for me, I wanted to fill the void immediately. I did this because unknowingly I was looking outside myself for love, approval and attention. It was later in life when I had several "failed" relationships in a row that I began to recognize a repeating pattern. *Note: It's important for me to mention that I don't believe any relationship is a "failure" if we grew (even a little bit) from it.* Not only did I attract men who exhibited varying degrees of disrespect, I attracted four alcoholics in a row! Being someone who is a very occasional drinker, I was attracting my polar opposite in order to provide a classroom for me to learn in. Excessive drinking was not on my list of pluses and at first notice, I should have bailed. However, my need for love, approval and attention would allow me to be sucked in by their good looks, charm and/or affection, and I would ignore the oftentimes very obvious red flags.

At that time in my life, after one relationship ended, I truly believed I was healed and ready to begin a new one because *I wasn't the problem!* Or so I told myself. But alas…I was the problem! It was I who was repeating a pattern. It was I who was the common denominator. The energy I was emitting was attracting the same type of relationship over and over again. I hadn't learned my lesson. Even though I felt strong and justified in eventually ending the relationships, I was not looking at myself and the potential reasons *why I* kept attracting the same type of man. My ego (false self) felt so justified in blaming the man, it didn't even occur to me that *I* may have been the problem! My justifications were all an ego-driven façade that kept me stuck and repeatedly drove me back into familiar territory. What is filtered through the ego is never correct. However, I did not know that at the time. Since I had not recognized and healed *my* portion of the relationship's dysfunction, the lessons were not learned. Furthermore, what is not healed will become our backpack and we will continue to carry our "stuff" into each consecutive relationship unless or until we do the necessary work.

After my tsunami hit, I took two years off from romantic relationships. It was time to recreate myself. I didn't consciously choose the amount of time, it just happened that way. All I knew was that I had to get emotionally healthy so that I could stop this cycle once and for all and I was going to refrain from dating until I felt truly ready to stand in my power. Through prayer, meditation and spiritual study, I expanded and strengthened. I finally recognized that something inside of me was not allowing me to honor myself. I did not love or value myself. I began to realize that I had repeatedly ignored the warning signs in most of my relationships and I allowed the relationships to continue way longer than I should have. In the case of one particular man, from the first "You're a f******* bitch!" weeks into our relationship for calling him out on a lie, I should have told him to buzz off. Nowhere in my values did I condone lying or name calling. It was not only a red-flag, but a red planet! Instead I made excuses for his behavior so I didn't have to leave. Although it took a betrayal of this magnitude to wake me up, I am so grateful that it did. It ignited a fire of determination to discover and heal the wounded Kristen, because I never wanted to fall for this illusion again.

At first my singledom felt weird and uncomfortable because it was out of my character and my conditioned mind pattern. I had never gone very long without a romantic relationship, but with each month that passed and with my primary focus on healing myself, I soon realized how serving it was and I began to welcome the time it took. Instead of filling the void with another distraction (romantic partner), I set course to nurture and love myself so I could again join the dating world (if and when I chose to) from a new, powerful place of self-respect and confidence.

What I uncovered upon deep reflection and exercises:

A. I had very little love and honor for myself.
B. I did not have firm guidelines as to what is acceptable and unacceptable in a relationship.
C. I would attach to the positive aspects of a man while ignoring the negatives.
D. I would launch into a deep attraction based on what little I knew of the person.
E. I did not listen to my intuition and ignored obvious warning signs.
F. I had great difficulty standing in my power (boundary setting) because my foundation was weak.

G. I worked to make him love me rather than focusing on whether I could love him.

With the help of these behaviors, the results were always painful. I would feel worse *within* a relationship than without! It was a profound spiritual lightning bolt when I finally realized, that *someone was not better than no one*. I even concluded in retrospect that several of those relationships would have never even begun if I knew then what I know now. I would have been turned off immediately. It was a humbling and healing awareness.

When we finally realize we must release the "need" to have someone in our lives at the expense of our well-being, we are finally on the right path for empowerment. The outcome we are striving for is to be the emotionally healthiest we can be *prior* to entering a new relationship. Oftentimes, this core healing can only be done when one is single because we don't have the distraction from self that we have when we are in a relationship. Since a doormat typically puts all her efforts into pleasing her partner, aloneness is imperative in the beginning while the healing happens and empowerment grows. This doesn't mean we wait until we are perfect to begin another relationship, because "perfect" will never happen. It means that after we have spent sufficient time on our healing work and have healed the best we are capable of *at this time*, then can we consider dating again.

Eventually we might actually require a relationship to uncover and heal a little further - perhaps a fine-tuning of what we have learned and are practicing. But for now, it is important to fight the urge to fill the void immediately and instead refocus all that energy on you! Consider this time a gift from God. We will know when we are ready to date again when our confidence has risen significantly and the constant, obsessive need for a relationship no longer exists. We will start to recognize that our thoughts and feelings regarding a relationship have changed considerably. A relationship will become a **bonus** to our life rather than a "need for happiness." Without the veil of need, our moral code and relationship standards become crystal clear. We will approach the relationship from more of an "observer" point of view rather than a "begging" point of view. Our healed heart and mind allows us to notice what we may not have ever noticed before. We are then in a better position to decide if this person is right for us, rather than us trying so hard to be right for this person.

The Exit Interview

At the end of a relationship, it is vitally important to conduct an exit interview prior to moving on to the next one. During this time, we process through the relationship by looking at all angles- his side and our side. We locate the places where we need transformation and then do the work required to achieving it. It can go something like this:

1. Out of all the broken portions of the relationship(s), what parts are mine to own and what parts are not mine to own?

   Note: Be very mindful here. Be careful not to own the whole demise as yours or contrarily play the blame game and allow it all to be the other person's fault. Even if 80% of the demise was theirs, you still hold 20% or vice versa. ***Your percentage could be exactly the lesson you need to lift you up and out of this pattern forever.***

2. What parts of myself am I seeking to fill up by the presence and attention of another person? Be willing to be 100% raw and real. What you discover you are wanting/needing from your partner is *exactly* what you are not giving to yourself.

   > Note: If you have trouble answering this question, consider consulting an empowerment coach or trusted, honest friend (a truth teller). This is not the time to be afraid of what you might discover. If possible, avoid examining with another "pleaser". Chances are he/she may be afraid to hurt your feelings and this would only serve to keep you stuck longer.

3. Where have I been out of integrity with myself? What are the places in me that are desperately trying to be heard that I have been ignoring? Where have I compromised my values and moral code for another?

4. What is the common denominator on my part in all of my past relationships? I.e. Inability to stand in own power, lack of confrontation, jealousy, control issues, manipulation, lack of vulnerability, protective walls, insecurities etc.

After discovering the places in yourself that need work, it's imperative to get busy doing it! You can heal yourself through a discipline of workshops, coaching sessions, talk-therapy with friends, meditation and prayer, books, seminars and/or mentors. We each learn differently. It's not *how* you do the work, but simply that you do it! Remember, you deserve the most beautifully fulfilling relationship, and it starts right now.

* * *

When we stay attached to another out of fear or desperation, we are only hurting ourselves. Allowing others to have space in our lives when they clearly do not honor us is a sure path to self-esteem destruction and yet another unhealthy relationship. We must be willing to love and honor ourselves first and foremost! It's about keeping the want or desire for a partner, but releasing the energy of "need". When we do this, we are telling the Universe we are deeply worthy and to please present to us people who will treat us the way we deserve – with support, love, respect and honor. When we heal ourselves, *our* vibration rises considerably. When we are buzzing at a higher frequency, we will be repelled by those who are vibrating at lower ones, therefore, not connecting with them in the first place and potentially starting something that would only end in pain. This entire concept is not only true for romantic relationships; it holds true for all relationships in our lives. The better you are connected to mind, body and spirit, the odds increase exponentially of you finding people of outstanding character to share your life with.

I understand how difficult it can be to let someone go. I know it may even spark feelings inside that they left because there is something wrong with you. How about choosing a new perspective - a perspective of healing and empowerment? People come and people go. It's all part of our journey. To hold onto someone who wants to leave or is treating us poorly is only blocking the doorway of what new and better experience/person the Universe will bring. Allow yourself or others to leave with love - no resentment, anger or bitterness. Then say YES to what wonderful new adventure is coming your way. Your job is to keep your heart open and allow God to do the rest!

Thoughts to Ponder: *Where have I stayed in relationships in order to not be alone? Do I feel as though*

I need a relationship to make me "happy"? Am I looking outside myself for the love, approval and attention I am not giving myself? Do I feel a sense of "need" to have a relationship or would it simply be a bonus in my life?

Set the Intention: *I am a unique and brilliant expression of God. I am amazing and beautiful in all ways. I deserve, as do all of God's children, a mutually loving and respectful relationship. I take good care and protection of myself and allow in only partners and friends who treat me with respect and honor. And so it is.*

Chapter Nine

Boundaries - Teach Others How to Treat You

"Remember, you are the most important person in your life. Until we begin to value ourselves enough to meet our own needs, we can't expect others around us to do it. Take it one step at a time." –Louise L. Hay

Our job as an empowered individual is to learn what is important to us and how to set and uphold appropriate boundaries. In doing this, we are teaching others how to treat us. We are making it very clear where our lines are so that our people are not guessing what it is we need or want nor are we carrying around extra baggage because we failed to take care of ourselves.

Standing in our power requires us to let go of the need for others to like us and instead stand committed to honoring ourselves first. Every day we have multiple opportunities to teach others what is acceptable to us. We communicate our boundaries (or lack of) through our behaviors and language thus setting the tone of the relationship. When two personalities join in a relationship (either platonic or romantic) they each bring with them a set of fears, ideas, beliefs and conditioned behaviors and patterns. Each will show up in a way that will communicate their individual values and where they are emotionally and physically. Both parties then have the opportunity to determine what works and what does not. We are responsible for whom and what is acceptable in our lives and by establishing boundaries and maintaining them, we are clearly showing others how we are protecting and defending our beloved self.

Setting boundaries can seem quite intimidating and frightening at first. The fear may be so strong for some people, that it inhibits them from taking the stand that could actually prove serving for both parties. We fear we may let someone down, hurt someone's feelings, make someone angry, or cause them to dislike us. We make their feelings a priority over our own. In turn, we justify to ourselves with innumerable reasons why we are not choosing to set a boundary. We sabotage our own lives because we are so afraid of rocking the boat and potentially losing another's love and approval. Oftentimes, we subconsciously feel we are not deserving of better treatment and/or we are afraid of being alone. Allowing others to treat us poorly is unacceptable any way we view it. An empowered person understands the purpose behind boundary setting and knows that boundaries are actually saying:

I am valuable. My opinions are valuable. My life is valuable. To be with me is to honor and respect me as I, too, will equally honor and respect you.

I am well aware firsthand this can be a mighty tough area for a doormat! We are so used to being "nice" and accepting of others' behaviors that we have no idea how to even begin. We may attempt to instill an occasional boundary, but our lack of self-worth often inhibits us from following through. Most often we feel guilt like we have done something terribly wrong. Trust me when I say, you are not alone. Right now is the precise moment to **stop, recognize** this conditioned behavioral pattern, and **start** the process of change. You are the only one who can break this pattern and begin to teach others how to love you best. It's all about creating and building relationships that are honoring and respecting of the person you are by openly and unabashedly communicating what is acceptable through words and action.

What Boundaries Are and Are Not:

- Boundaries are a way of setting limits for those in our lives that clearly shows them what is unacceptable for us.
- Boundaries are about self-worth - not selfishness.
- Boundaries are set with clear communication. If we do not express our limits, the other person has no way of knowing.
- Boundaries are essential for healthy relationships.
- Boundaries require action to back them up if words are not enough.

The Power of 'No'

"A 'No' uttered from the deepest conviction is better than a 'Yes' merely uttered to please, or worse, to avoid trouble." – Mohandas Gandhi

Since doormat-hood can oftentimes run parallel with codependency - *placing a lower priority on one's own needs, while being excessively preoccupied with the needs of others* - it can be extremely difficult, if not fully non-existent, for a doormat to say 'No'. Since we are on a journey to self-empowerment and deeper self-love, it is important to recognize one's own behavior and the possible reasons behind this lack of boundary support. *A powerful 'No' comes when we do not have any hidden beliefs as to why we are unworthy of a 'No'.* These are the places that need to be uncovered in order to truly heal and become a fully empowered individual. It's important to have inquiry into why we are refraining from setting a boundary. Start by asking yourself the following questions:

1. What is stopping me from setting or supporting this boundary? What am I afraid of?

2. What belief or core thought am I believing that is holding me back from claiming respect?
3. Are the answers to the above questions absolutely true?

Once we determine our hold back (fear), we then know the precise location where we need healing in order to be able to stand powerfully (without guilt) behind our boundary. Learning to recognize the limiting belief will help you move quickly past the guilt and allow for a new and better feeling to help you hold your line. Below is a list of commonly held beliefs (the lies) that can keep us from a healthy 'No' and the turn-around of that belief (the truth).

I am a jerk or a bitch if I say 'No'. Truth- Others may push back when we set our boundaries; however, any name calling, judgments or guilting are an attempt on the other person's part to control us. We must understand this mechanism and be strong enough to stand in our power. If we are calling ourselves names, judging or guilting, we must stop the sabotaging behaviors immediately and remember to always be gentle and respectful to self.

I am guilty when I say 'No' or set boundaries. We

mistakenly believe that we are doing the wrong thing. Our lack of worthiness shines full force when we don't set appropriate boundaries. Truth- You are a valuable person whose birthright is to take care of you the best you can and to teach others how best to treat you. There is no room or reason for guilt while protecting and respecting your sacred self. You matter!

I am selfish when I say 'No' or set boundaries. Since we have a history of always saying 'Yes', when we first begin to value and honor ourselves with a well-placed 'No', it may feel like we are being selfish. Truth- *There is no selfishness in self-love.* To take care of oneself is an act of Love. Love resides within the service of God. Where God is, there is only Love and where there's Love, there can be no selfishness. When we take care of ourselves, we actually show up in the world a happier, peaceful and more rounded individual now capable of giving our best selves to our people.

It's my job/role to say 'Yes'. When we put ourselves in a box that our role (mother, friend, teacher, confidant, career position) requires every, tiny piece of ourselves, we are completely misaligned with our purpose, passions and self. Truth- Our job is to take care of self *while* we perform in our chosen roles. To go overboard in either one is to create great disharmony and distress within our mind, body and spirit. Boundaries are about designing and upholding a balance of responsibility and self.

I will lose another's love if I set this boundary. This is probably the most common and biggest false belief we tell ourselves in our attempt to set and maintain healthy boundaries. Truth- The people who truly love us may indeed push back when we begin setting boundaries because they will not be used to the new program. However, they will eventually begin to respect our lines and actually grow a deeper respect for us. We may also become a leader in their eyes- someone they can turn to for inspiration. Contrarily, the ones who are in relationships with us just to "get" something might fall out of our lives. Let them fall away. One of the goals of this journey is to create a community of equal support, respect and love within our circle of family and friends. The ones who do not respect and honor our truths and our path have no business being in our community and we must be willing to release them with love.

Many times I hear from people how they have a hard time letting people go. Somehow we believe that to lose someone from our life, is inadvertently saying that *we were not good enough*. We will mistakenly personalize them leaving our lives as our fault. This is simply untrue and this belief system will only keep us stuck. However, fascinatingly our consciousness begins to shift as we strengthen and uphold ourselves. We naturally begin to lose attachment to the "takers" in our lives and begin to understand that our energy is now vibrating at a different frequency. What once may have worked, may not work any longer. We will also begin to see that when one person leaves our lives, a space is created for a new person of equal vibration to enter. There is nothing sad about that.

How Boundaries Serve Both Parties

"An intimate relationship is one in which neither party silences, sacrifices, or betrays the self and each party expresses strength and vulnerability, weakness and competence in a balanced way." - Harriet Lerner

A great paradox to setting personal boundaries is it can actually serve both parties. Our boundaries and clear sense of self can shine light on others' dependencies and controlling behaviors and potentially start them on their own healing path. It's important to remember that a lot of what others are doing is through their conditioned patterns and they may not even be aware of how they are coming across. When they begin to receive the message enough, they will eventually have little choice but to take a good hard look at themselves. By honoring *ourselves first*, we are inadvertently showing them a piece within *themselves* that potentially needs a new perspective. By standing in our truth and maintaining our boundaries, we are very likely creating a win-win situation for both parties.

A couple years back, a very important person in my life was in an unhealthy relationship. She was very confused and hurt by her partner's actions. We would talk for hours and hours regarding her situation. I would repeatedly give her tools to help navigate through her situation but it seemed she just wanted to stay stuck in the injustice and drama of her story. Since we were close, I had virtually no time constraints as to when she could call me and quite often it was at 2 a.m.! (I created this by constantly being available whenever she needed me) As time went on, I noticed that our conversations went around and around. She was not moving forward and I was getting exhausted! It took me a bit to come to this conclusion, but I decided to start setting boundaries with her. I gently explained that I had given her all the tools I had and that it was time for her to work through it on her own. I would still talk with her of course, but I now had time limits and the 2 a.m. conversations were no longer allowed. That's when the miracle happened!

At first she was upset with me for setting a boundary on our conversations, but eventually, she came back to me with miraculous insights! When she no longer had me to distract her, she was able to find her own strength, design a forward movement and empower *herself*! When I finally set a firm boundary for *my* well-being, it turned out to be the best thing for her as well! Soon thereafter, she broke up with her toxic partner and found herself, her passion and her joy once again. My need to play the "rescuer" was not only enabling her, but exhausting me. It is not always true that we will be able to see the rewards this clearly, but it is important for us to recognize that boundary setting is indeed a behavior placed out of love.

Disciplining the Mind

"To enjoy good health, to bring true happiness to one's family, to bring peace to all, one must first discipline and control one's own mind. If a man can control his mind he can find the way to Enlightenment, and all wisdom and virtue will naturally come to him."
-Buddha

As with all the practices in this book, learning to discipline our mind is how we will create great change in our lives. With any great accomplishment, there is always a firm discipline in place. The road to self-empowerment doesn't happen with a sprinkle of pixie dust and a wish on the wind. It takes courage, dedication, time commitment and fortitude to stay on task. We must truly **want** change in our lives in order to **create** change. Although this subchapter would have been perfect placed anywhere in this book, I felt it best served in the boundary chapter because setting boundaries will take immense discipline. We will need to constantly be reminding ourselves of our worth and be vigilant in catching our defeating thoughts. By first becoming aware that we have conditioned patterns of doing things, we are better able to recognize when those patterns come up. We will begin to recognize and feel the uneasiness associated with our doormat behavior. Once recognized we must then have a "go to" plan of how we are to handle them as they come up. The most important piece to setting and upholding appropriate boundaries is to affirm our worth.

Below are a few affirming statements (mind disciplining) when we find ourselves feeling weak and tempted to renege on our boundary:

- I am worthy of the space I am attempting to create with this boundary.
- My time is valuable and I am valuable. I will choose wisely how I spend my time.
- I am not responsible for another's feelings or life. They are responsible for their own.
- My job is to take care of me so that I may take great care of others.
- It is completely acceptable to have my own needs, desires and passions. I am not hurting another by spending time with myself or on myself.
- I am happier when I take care of myself and I give this gift to myself and my family.

- Another's attempt at manipulation has nothing to do with how I feel about myself.
- I cannot control another's behavior. I can only set a well-placed boundary.

To become great at anything, it takes practice. Disciplining our mind to push out defeating thoughts will take some time. Please be gentle with yourself in the process. How long it takes will depend on how diligent one understands the necessity and wants the change. What we focus on we create. If one puts great focus on her self-worth and desire for peace in her life, the discipline becomes easier. Be mindful that you matter.

How to Recognize When It's Boundary Time - Change the Situation

"Your personal boundaries protect the inner core of your identity and your right to choices." – David Richo

Boundaries can be described as setting limits in our relationships. It can be anything from hanging up the phone with someone when you are too tired to keep talking, opting out of a night of partying, removing yourself from toxic people or not allowing someone to borrow money who never repays the debt. When we discover ourselves in a situation we do not like, we have one of three choices to make: to *change* the situation, to *leave* the situation or to *accept* the situation. Typically a disempowered person will either accept the situation (passively) or leave it (aggressively) because either way may *appear to be easier* than pushing uncomfortable limits. Although accepting and leaving can be appropriate options when shaped from a healthy assessment, it's important to know, great change comes from refusing to take the path of least resistance. An empowered person will first attempt *to change the situation by changing herself* to see if this is the answer.

It is fairly easy to recognize where a boundary needs to be placed by observing our emotions and discovering the root thoughts of them. Our emotions are lamp posts illuminating places in us where we may feel disrespected or mistreated. Anger is usually one of the first emotions we feel because many other emotions tend to hide under the "anger umbrella" – fear, frustration, pain, confusion etc. When we begin to feel a lower emotion, seemingly caused by another's words or behaviors, we must be willing to recognize it, find its core (the reason behind the emotion) and design and implement a healthy boundary. This is the model for any boundary no matter how big or how small.

I remember a time when a partner was pushing himself into all areas of my life. I hardly had any time for myself, my children's needs or my passions. I could feel myself feeling frustrated at first and later it turning into anger. I was beginning to feel very turned off toward him. I attempted to set boundaries, but I did so in a passive, overly sweet way and when he pushed back just a little, I folded. My conditioned mind was telling me I'd be turning my back on someone who needed me thus mistakenly believing he was my responsibility (self-guilt). I amped up the boundary by becoming more firm. Again, he pushed and I folded. As time went on, I was really feeling annoyed and angry. I set another boundary and he pushed A-gain! What I learned was that the problem was not he, it was I. I was not standing firm in my boundaries. Through my own egoic (fearful) thinking, I was not supporting (self-love) my own needs. I decided at that time that I needed some space to sort through the "whys" of my behavior. Once I did the work, I was able to go back to the situation with personal integrity and take the necessary steps (removing defeating thoughts/mind discipline) in order to stand strong in my boundary. The relationship shifted immediately and once again it served not only me, but him as well. In turn, he was then able to look more closely into why he was constantly pushing himself into my life and then do the necessary work on himself to heal his behavior.

When Boundaries Are Not Enough- Leave the Situation

"There is no real ending. It's just the place where you stop the story." –Frank Herbert

To allow people to continually abuse and/or treat us poorly is unacceptable in any form. If firm boundaries are not working, we must consider leaving the situation for good or until a marked shift occurs. It is our sole responsibility to teach others how to treat us and it is their responsibility to listen to and respect our boundaries. Unfortunately, we have people in our lives who, no matter what, will not treat us in an acceptable way. *Being willing* to lose the relationship is half the battle. Once we truly know that we will be better off without that person in our lives, it is much easier to move on. It's important to note that sometimes letting go isn't about removing others completely from our lives. By making a conscious/Spirit-based decision based on our inner knowing and the facts of the relationship, we can make a very healthy choice for us.

I had a friend for ten years. We were very close and did a lot together. Over those ten years, she did several things to me that were completely unacceptable. One example was when she followed my husband down the hall into our bedroom and while wearing a miniskirt and five inch heels, she threw her foot high up on our wall to keep him from exiting the room. I happened to walk around the corner at that precise moment. All I could spit out was, "What are you doing?!" She laughed it off as a joke and walked away. Being the doormat I was, I chose to ignore what happened and excused it away in order not to confront an uncomfortable situation. It didn't help that my ex was very uncomfortable as well and asked me to drop it. So I did. It wasn't until another act of betrayal did I finally make the decision to *leave the situation*. In that precise moment, I decided that to keep her in my life was more painful than to have her out of it and I ended the friendship. I later learned that the things she did to me, she was also doing to her other friends as well. I was no exception to her unhealthy behavior no matter how close we were.

What happens when we don't want to let go by leaving the situation? Well, we have two choices: One, we can accept them as they are and stay in the relationship (with the understanding that *we are choosing* to stay without change) or two, we can come to a compromise regarding the subject of distress. With either choice, be prepared to change some aspect of *you* in order to uphold your half of the new agreement. If you decide to allow the behavior, it would be unfair to keep bringing it up. Consistency is key here if you are truly working towards a shift. If both of you choose to compromise, remember that there is still the possibility that the other person will default on his/her side of the deal. Be prepared for when or if that happens and have a plan in place. Only you can decide what works for you and what does not. Whatever you choose, it is still ultimately *your* actions that will determine your future.

In determining our action, the question we must ask ourselves is:

Is it worth it to deal with this person's behavior in order to keep the relationship or is it simply too painful, unacceptable or disrespectful to keep them in my circle?

I feel it imperative to add that in the case of physical and/or extreme emotional abuse, there are no exceptions. As the wise Maya Angelou states, "When people show you who they are the first time, believe them." Abuse of any kind should not be accepted at any cost. If they did it once, they will continue to do it and it will only continue to deplete your self-esteem and confidence more and more. I implore you to please locate an association near you that can assist you in leaving the environment. There are numbers of agencies designed to handle cases of domestic abuse and I highly encourage you to seek the help available to get you to safety. **You are your #1 priority.**

A Shift in Perception - Accept the Situation

"God grant me the serenity to accept the things I cannot change; courage to change the things I can; and wisdom to know the difference."
–The Serenity Prayer

Setting hard lines with people isn't always the answer. At times, we need to go within and look for the places where we are not acting or thinking from Love (compassion and forgiveness) and then do the work to consciously bring Love into the situation. There are going to be times we perceive a boundary is needed, when in fact a change in perception is what's called for. How does one know when it is appropriate to accept the situation or when a change in perception will best serve? The answer comes through honest inquiry:

- Am I accepting this situation because I don't want to rock the boat?

   *Boundary needed

- Am I accepting this situation because I am too fearful to state my truth?

   *Boundary needed

- Am I accepting this situation because I am fearful of being judged/rejected/not accepted?

   *Boundary needed

   OR

- Am I accepting this situation because I have done my part to set boundaries, uphold them and because leaving is not a possibility, I will work on my Love Skills (compassion, forgiveness and understanding) in order to find a peaceful way to coexist in this relationship?

*Change in perception needed

Through true self-evaluation, we are able to break down the dense, heavy atmosphere of a situation into smaller bits so that we may see more clearly. When we see things as they truly are without the lens of anger, contempt, fear or resentment, we are better able to find an appropriate forward movement. Sometimes the best forward movement may not be a boundary, but a shift in one's perspective.

There was a woman who repeatedly set boundaries with her elderly father. Her father was from an old-world, European background and would not heed her boundaries regarding her parenting. She wasn't in a position to leave the situation, nor did she really want to. She loved him dearly. Through honest self-evaluation, she decided that if she had more compassion for his backstory and understood his thinking better, she wouldn't have the huge emotional reaction she always had when he crossed her lines. She continued to do her part to keep her lines in place;

however, if he occasionally crossed them, she chose to default to understanding, compassion and forgiveness rather than anger and contempt. She would state her truth and boundary and then let go. Prior to spending time with him, she grounded herself in strength, love and compassion. Her entire demeanor around him changed because she was no longer walking into the scene ready to defend and fight. As time went on, she let go of his judgment and interference and all at once, he stopped doing it!

Boundaries are an essential part of doormat recovery. They will take discipline, practice and a deep desire for a more peaceful life. So much can be learned by both parties when an appropriate boundary is set and upheld. To keep quiet is to perpetuate the same result in relationships and to continue to disrespect your most valuable loved one… you. Remember, boundaries are not based in selfishness. They are actions expressed through a conscious connection with our self-love, self-worth and self-respect. You are worth it!

Thoughts to Ponder: *Am I upset with someone else's behavior and I have not spoken up about it? What is my* *reason for not setting a boundary? Would it serve my highest good to set a boundary with this person?*

Set the Intention: *I am worthy and deserving of loving and respectful treatment from the people I have relationships with. I attract people of high integrity into my life. I am willing to speak my truth when someone is not honoring me. And so it is.*

If you are interested in contacting Kristen for personal coaching/mentoring, group talks or would simply like to stay current with her articles, blogs and Facebook posts, please follow the links below:

www.sweetempowerment.com

www.facebook.com/sweetempowermentlifecoaching

CPSIA information can be obtained at www.ICGtesting.com
Printed in the USA
BVOW07s1918211014

371761BV00001B/4/P

9 781452 519036